Can You Hear Me Now?

Finding My Voice in a System That Stole It

Angela McCrimmon

Aurora Books
Eugene, Oregon, USA

Aurora Books, an imprint of Eco-Justice Press, L.L.C.

Aurora Books
P.O. Box 5409 Eugene, OR 97405
www.ecojusticepress.com

Can You Hear Me Now?: Finding My Voice in a System That Stole It
By Angela McCrimmon

Cover by David Diethelm, Eco-Justice Press

Library of Congress Control Number: 2016941155
ISBN 978-1-945432-00-2

This Book Is Dedicated To Louise Davidson:
It takes a very special person to look out on a bed of thistles
believing they will find lavender and bluebell underneath…
if they just don't give up searching.

XX

Chapters

Introduction

I vaguely remember my eyes flickering open as they responded to a sudden burst of light. It took a few moments for my eyes and my brain to act in synchronisation but an even longer moment to remind my heart to reignite for breath. When they eventually came together my stomach hit the floor realising the bright light was that of a flashlight and the delay was not dissimilar to the moment when you wake in the night to the relief that you have awoken from a dream. That moment when you are caught between the line of your subconscious and the line of reality. The problem was that I wasn't awakening from a dream. I was in the midst of a nightmare and the most terrifying part was that I was fully awake. I had been admitted to the Psychiatric Ward....again!

I spent many nights lying in the room, often awake for consecutive nights listening to other patients breathe peacefully as their medication brought about the sedation each of us longed for. I could hear staff congregated at the Nurses Station which was strategically placed at the top of the corridor so that on one side they could monitor the male patients and the other side the female ones. I often heard Nurses talking and always found their laughter somehow intensified the distress I found myself in. Almost as if it were adding an air of cruelty to the fact they were on one side of the desk and I was on the other. In hindsight I'm quite

(Cont'd)

certain this theory was unrealistic but with certain staff I never always had the reassurance that I was mistaken. Paranoia on my part perhaps more than an intentional desire to cause hurt but nevertheless, it was present.

I hadn't meant things to get this out of control. I spent so much of my time gripping on for dear life and sometimes the only thing that kept me holding on was that millisecond where you let go entirely in an attempt to attain a better, stronger grasp. The problem was this millisecond of freefall versus the majority of stability had become confused. Somewhere along the road the equilibrium had been upset and the exhaustion I felt for the energy it took to maintain my grasp often engulfed my being. I found my comfort in self-harm which in that moment helped….further down the road it almost cost me my limbs.

I've met many kinds of people in my life but I can confidently say there is one category that had the ability to crush my heart and damage my soul more than any other. The Medical Profession.

Writing has become my most powerful, healing tool and through my words I am able to connect the dots between my head and my heart. I promised myself that I was going to take every thought and every feeling I'd ever had and offer it to the people who need to understand them more than anyone. Medical Professionals….other patients and their loved ones…but above all, the person who needs to understand more than any other is quite simply myself. It's my heart, my soul, my story.

I may not have the medical knowledge that Doctors do but surely I have one thing they don't? Experience.

Can you hear me now?

1
Fragile, Handle With Care

This is the beginning of my journey into the Mental Health System... the part when my thoughts and emotions would overwhelm me and the part when I realised I was different from other people. Other people seemed to float through life where I found myself struggling to even stay afloat. I could never have known these feelings would lead me into a System and a Diagnosis of Mental Illness that would follow me through life and destroy my world. I was officially "different."

MAYBE NOT TODAY

I know things will get better and I will be just fine,
I wake up in the morning and I long to see a sign,
A sign that things are changing, that joy is on its way,
I know I'll be alright......just maybe not today.

I know around the corner there could be so much in store,
I know that I must learn to shut that painful door,
Shut out all the feelings of sadness and despair,
I tell myself that one day those feelings won't be there.

I know that it's destructive to listen to my thoughts,
Sometimes they are good but mostly they are not,
Destroy the voice inside that says to self-destruct,
Listen to the one that says "please don't give up."

I know it's so irrational and doesn't make much sense,
I wish I knew what I must do to jump to my defence,
It feels like I've no choice in the damage that I do,
The choice always lies with me so that cannot be true.

I know my life is scary for uncertainty lives on,
I just need reassurance that these feelings will be gone,
I need to face the morning believing when I say,
"Things will be alright.....just maybe not today."

Angela McCrimmon

I HIDE

I hide my broken heart in the actions that you see,
If you would look beyond them I know you would find me.
I hide my tear stained face in the make-up that I wear,
If you'd look underneath then you would find me there.

I hide my anxiety when I cancel all our plans,
If you would see around it you would see just who I am.
I hide my deep sadness with the smile upon my face,
If you were down there with me you would find me in that place.

I hide my lack of confidence by playing the class clown,
You don't know I'm crying when there's no-one else around.
I hide my self-hatred with long sleeve after sleeve,
For if you saw what's under them I think that you would leave.

I hide my fear of judgement by saying "I don't care,"
If you could read between the lines you'd see it isn't fair.
I hide my own opinion by saying "I don't mind,"
It's just my personality, the "people pleasing" kind.

I hide what I am thinking by staring into space,
If you could be in my day-dreams you'd soon see what I face.
I hide away my madness, I make you think I'm fun,
I feel so exhausted entertaining everyone.

I push away the people, the ones I should keep close,
I make it hard to love me yet it's what I need the most.

YOU AND ME

You can tell the story but I read between the lines,
You can use direction but I can see the signs,
You use explanation but I can't understand,
You can walk alone where I reach for your hand.

You apologise at the parts I can forgive,
You will fight the fear while I will fight to live,
You reveal the things that I try so hard to hide,
You will speak out loud all the things I say inside.

You can feel excitement where all I feel is dread,
You can see fruition, I'm incomplete instead,
You reach for tomorrow while I'm barely holding on,
You seem so bewildered at what I've known so long.

You can float through life at the points I almost drown,
You are flying high when I'm still on the ground,
You meet expectation where I expect to fail,
You are on a journey at the points where I derail.

You see disappointment where I can see success,
You see grand endeavours where I see more is less,
You wish for the future, I wish for just today,
I guess our worlds are different and I guess that that's okay.

Angela McCrimmon

SMILE

You asked me today if I was feeling sad, I smiled and turned away,
I thought to myself that I always do, I just cannot hide it today,
I feel so tired, so weary and worn, I've no strength left inside,
It took all I had to get out the door when everything told me to hide.

I don't even have the words to explain, well actually that isn't true,
I've many words swimming around they just cannot float to you,
It feels as if I am looking out on an island so far from shore,
I'm confused and don't know who I am, I don't know much anymore.

I'm standing here and yet I couldn't be much further away,
You ask me if I'm alright, I tell you that I am okay,
I don't think you'd know what to say if my answer was sincere,
I guess I feel that the words I have are the kind you don't want to hear.

I'm trying so hard to listen yet I cannot hear you at all,
You look to me like a giant for I feel so tiny and small,
I'm trying to keep composure but who am I fooling right now?
I long to let my guard down but I'm mindful I don't know how.

I don't think I'll ever explain, not sure if there's even a need,
I seem to get by okay so don't worry you don't have to heed,
There is no need to ask me how I am doing today,
For I know that I will only smile and then I will turn away.

NOTE TO MIND

Where do you go when you are not here?
Sometimes you're away for days,
Your absence leaves me with such fear,
So scared in a million ways.

You give me no sign that you'll be gone,
You just up and walk away,
You make it clear that we don't belong,
Together at the end of the day.

Some people ask me how you are,
Embarrassed I say, "Oh, fine,"
The truth is that you seem so far,
You do this to me every time.

I know sometimes I probably do,
Cause you to get up and leave,
There are times I get so angry with you,
To hurt you is all I achieve.

Sometimes I close my eyes and pray,
That soon you will come back home,
I always hope there will come a day,
When you won't leave me here alone.

So where do you go when you're not here?
I beg you to hear my plea,
I need you Mind for I am in fear,
When you are not here with me.

Angela McCrimmon

BROKEN

Some learn easy but I learn hard,
Some people keep what I discard,
To win I guess I had to lose,
To be select I had to choose.

I had to mature and just accept,
Sometimes the answer is "not yet,"
Some things in life you just can't rush,
My dreams I know will sometimes crush.

I had to admit my life was a lie,
To build the new, the old must die,
To prove I really did want more,
I had to firmly close that door.

It seems I had to first destroy,
To find what truly brought me joy,
To feel the triumph life could bring,
I had to lose most everything.

The lesson learned each time again,
"If things don't change they'll stay the same,"
If I don't stand up for myself,
Then I'm to blame, no-one else.

I learned the person that I could be,
Was found when I was "fixing" me,
The voice that tells me every day,
"You're a little broken...and that's okay."

GOOD MORNING

Good morning, hello, yes how do you do?
I believe we've already met,
I'm the one who lives inside of you,
Lest you should ever forget.

I'm in control, I assure you it's true,
I will always be your friend,
From the moment you wake 'til the day is through,
Right through til its very end.

Sometimes you're nasty, you tell me to go,
So I retreat for a little while,
Give it some time, I've no doubt I know,
In the end you will make me smile.

You will make me smile for I know it's true,
I laugh while you wriggle and squirm,
I'm loyal and won't walk away from you,
It's me that makes you toss and turn.

I'll whisper gently you will hear my voice,
Even when you don't know I am there,
I'll help you see that it's not your choice,
Unconditional love I will care.

What makes you think you can do this alone?
What gives you the right to say?
You tell you would rather be alone,
You scream at me "PLEASE GO AWAY!!"

Don't worry, I know just to give you some time,
I know I'll make you understand,
Just stick with me, I'll make everything fine,
You just have to hold out your hand.

(Cont'd)

9

(Cont'd)

No need to reach far as I'm always so close,
It's "our secret" I know you will keep,
Just shut out the world and don't let them know,
Just tell them that you fell asleep.

Don't tell them it's because I get angry with you,
How dare you try to walk away!
How dare you question if my words are true,
For your doubt I will make you pay.

I'm expensive you know, money can't buy,
I'll cost you so many things,
I've taken your courage, so don't even try,
I'll take over everything.

Good morning, hello, yes how do you do?
I know that we've met before,
Anxiety's my name and you know that it's true,
I'm waiting outside your front door.

REALITY

I'm a little weary, I might need some sleep,
Reality, I'm exhausted and I can't even speak.
I am feeling fine, yes sure I am okay,
Reality, I'm screaming but being drowned out anyway.

I'm feeling so excited, I can barely wait,
Reality, I feel sick as I draw near to the date.
I'm a little sad, I feel a little low,
Reality, I'm desperate I just don't want it to show.

Everything is good, it's all going right to plan,
Reality, I've no idea just where the hell I am!
I look so happy and I smile all the time,
Reality, it's just another trick of looking fine.

Hey, I'm not so bothered, it wasn't meant to be,
Reality, Devastated! It was only meant for me.
I tell you where I'm heading, my five year plan is clear,
Reality, I'm lost and there's a chance I won't be here.

I'm feeling rather stressed, I'll maybe have a bath,
Reality, I'm crippled by anxiety and its wrath.
I wish that you could see me and inside this head of mine,
Reality, that girl you see....she only works part-time.

Angela McCrimmon

DAVID.....LOST LOVE

They ask me if I'm married and I always choose to say,
"Yes I surely am, he just can't be here today,"
I don't feel the need to tell them for they don't need to know,
The truth is my Darling that you left me long ago.

I don't want them to feel awkward or take them by surprise,
From where I am standing I'm not telling any lies,
You're always right beside me but for now we are apart,
I don't live a single day without you in my heart.

I know they often wonder why they don't ever see,
This man that I speak of when he belongs to me,
So many parties and they see me there alone,
I know they want to question why you've left me on my own.

I'm happy for I know that you're with me day and night,
I hear you reassure me that I'm going to be alright,
I hear your voice so clearly whispering my name,
We sleep in separate rooms yet together all the same.

I'm proud you are my husband and I'm so proud to be your wife,
Forever you will be the only man to touch my life,
That's why I can stand here so solid and so strong,
Our love it is so "right" but the situation's wrong.

They ask me if I'm married and I always choose to say,
"Yes, I surely am, he just can't be here today,"
I know that if you could it is where you'd want to be,
Instead you're on the other side waiting there for me.

CHOICES

Why do I choose to sleep when others cannot wake?
They can make good choices where I just make mistakes,
They all have direction yet my journey is unmapped,
Some have plans in concrete but my only plan's "Adapt."

Why do I destroy what others can preserve?
Why do I accept much less than I deserve?
I have an understanding that this is how it is,
I fight a war of death while others fight to live.

Whenever there's discomfort I find my peace in pain,
When things are unfamiliar they somehow feel the same,
I lock myself in silence, I hide my trembling voice,
They can hear conviction when all I hear is noise.

I need to find acceptance of the fact I'm in denial,
Where many find employment, I am just on trial,
Each breath brings a challenge and I don't always win,
But the war I must never lose is one where I give in.

Angela McCrimmon

EXPLANATION

You say think of something happy instead,
But how can I run from these thoughts in my head?
They follow me everywhere that I go,
So much inside that you do not know.

To you it's an easy decision to make,
For me it's a giant step to take,
My heart feels what your eyes don't see,
Would you cope if you were me?

You say that I must get in line,
Prepare myself ahead of time,
If you could see how hard I try,
You'd maybe feel how much I cry.

I see no point so why explain?
You see an excuse and say I'm to blame,
I pin no blame for you don't see,
It's just the way life is for me.

So when you see I'm hit by the blues,
Please know it's not the journey I choose,
I'd gladly jump off at the nearest station,
It's not an excuse it's an explanation.

QUESTIONS

How do you find acceptance when you've only felt reject?
How do you find true love when your first love was neglect?
How do you ever find the thing you long for most?
The love of somebody when you only have their ghost.

How do you gain control of what's controlling you?
How do you show reality when pretending's what you do?
How do you undo a whole lifetime of such pain?
How do you find relief from all the madness in your brain?

How do you find your future when you're locked up in your past?
How do you find tomorrow when yesterday still lasts?
How do you tell the world the person that they know?
Is hurting so deep down and you don't know where to go.

I ask so many questions and I have a million more,
So terrified of ever walking through that door,
I'm barely hanging on and I don't know if I could,
Trust my injured soul in the hands of those I should.

I battle through each day then each long and lonely night,
I need to tell my story but I don't know what to write,
I need to find release from the shame inside my soul,
I pray someday I'll find my broken heart made whole.

Angela McCrimmon

I SEE

I see some content to live their life unwell,
I guess some have known no other way,
We all have our stories, some we cannot tell,
It doesn't mean we don't have much to say.

I see some so passive, life passes by,
Happy to watch it as it goes,
Not stopping for a moment to wonder why,
Questions yet no desire to know.

I see some so angry and so they do display,
Behaviour that so many will reject,
No real desire to find another way,
Or maybe they just haven't found it yet?

I see some regret, living with deep shame,
Replaying each mistake they ever made,
Cringing when somebody says their name,
Scars that with time might never fade.

I see some have hope though a little insecure,
Anticipating all that they could be,
I look a little harder and see that I am sure,
The reflection I am looking at is me.

SURVIVE

I won't pretend that I don't care because I care beyond belief,
I won't pretend that I'm okay because I'm lost amidst the grief,
I won't pretend it's easy because it's hard to be alive,
I won't pretend it doesn't hurt...but you know what?...I'll survive!

I won't pretend I'm happy because I know that I feel sad,
I won't pretend I'm "together" because I feel like I've gone mad,
I won't pretend I'm motivated because I know I've lost my drive,
I won't pretend that I'm not bruised...but you know what?...I'll survive!

I won't pretend I'm not angry because I know inside I am,
I won't pretend I can't forgive because I know inside I can,
I won't pretend I respect you for my respect has all but died,
I won't pretend it doesn't hurt...but you know what?...I'll survive!

Angela McCrimmon

BOXES

Everyone has their very own way,
They do what they do to survive,
Taken aback when I realised today,
This strategy got me through my life.

I'd taken each hurt and I'd taken each pain,
I'd locked them so tightly away,
No need to look at them ever again,
For they belonged to yesterday.

Each memory had its very own box,
I'd chosen to close the lid,
No need to ever look at the clock,
I hadn't realised that's what I did.

Whatever happens whatever unfolds,
I knew that I'd be okay,
I always knew that whatever life holds,
The thoughts I could take far away.

I realised the way that I'd learned to cope,
Was denial in a form of its own,
I thought that because I always had hope,
Didn't realise the pain I'd postpone.

I don't mean that I would ever forget,
For my memory was quite intact,
It's like somehow I could disconnect,
The path from my head to my heart.

I learned that I had to open each box,
I learned that given some time,
I found the way to somehow unlock,
So my heart and my head could entwine.

HAPPY BIRTHDAY

"Close your eyes, make a wish and don't tell anyone,"
I knew from the outside they thought I'm having fun,
I guess in a way I was because I knew what I must do,
Make my wish again, last years didn't come true.

I didn't wish for a pony, I didn't wish for a doll,
I didn't wish for a puppy, instead I wished I'd fall,
Not content with falling right here on the ground,
I wished to fall downstairs when no-one was around.

I didn't wish for money, I didn't wish for clothes,
I didn't want new shoes because I knew that none of those,
Could fill this empty feeling, the one I tried to hide,
I wished I'd fall off my bike as I peddled around outside.

I didn't wish for toys, I didn't wish for a game,
I didn't want a new book for I knew they were the same,
That none would bring more joy than the thing I hoped for most,
I wished I was invisible and I could be a scary ghost.

I didn't wish for pencils, I didn't wish for pens,
I didn't want a colouring book, I didn't want any of them,
I knew what my wish would be for I'd wished the same last year,
I wished that maybe next birthday I would not be here.

Angela McCrimmon

THE ART OF CONVERSATION

I can hear you're talking yet all of the while,
I haven't a clue so I nod and I smile,
I realise that there is an answer required,
When you pause for breath, your sentence expired.

I laugh when you laugh and I take my own cue,
I'm learning my lines while I'm watching you,
I'm taking direction from all that you say,
Secretly starring in my very own play.

I'm good in a crisis and quick to respond,
I'm here in the moment while looking beyond,
I'm one step ahead and I guess this is why,
My wit is the one thing money can't buy.

I listen intently so I can reply,
I look for instruction so I can comply,
Open-end questions are always a must,
When everything fails in these I can trust.

I try to engage even when I am bored,
No-one more wasted than the one who's ignored,
No-one more happy than the one who's in flow,
I'm aware of this so it's the one thing I'll show.

So next time you see me, nod and just smile,
Show me some kindness, stay for a while,
Give me the time like you haven't a clock,
For one moment please let me be more than a thought.

RAIN

They called it April showers for this was a sign,
A sure sign that spring was on its way,
A new lease of life this season would bring,
A time of new beginnings to convey.

They taught us very young each droplet from the sky,
Was sent to help the flowers grow,
Without the glistening rain the flowers would surely die,
Emerging from the soil to say hello.

The rain kept us cool when the sun was so hot,
"It's so close" I would hear the adults say,
I'd look around and think "So close to what??"
No cool air to circulate the day.

The rain made puddles, I'd watch the children splash,
I stood back afraid to join in,
For the puddles full of rain reminded me of wrath,
The kind of trouble I knew I was in.

The rain fell upon my face as I walked along,
Sadness fell and I remembered why,
So many years I thought that I'd done wrong,
And that rain was the tears I'd made God cry.

Angela McCrimmon

MAYBE

Maybe I will, maybe I won't,
Maybe I do, maybe I don't,
Maybe the answer I'll never say,
Maybe I'll choose to walk away.

Maybe I know, maybe I'll guess,
Maybe I care or couldn't care less,
Maybe I see much more than you do,
Maybe that's false or maybe it's true.

Maybe I laugh, maybe I cry,
Maybe I'll live, maybe I'll die,
Maybe I feel, maybe I'm numb,
Maybe I'm fooling everyone.

Maybe I'll go, maybe I'll stay,
Maybe I'll bow my head and pray,
Maybe I'll hide, maybe I'll seek,
Maybe I'm strong, maybe I'm weak.

Maybe I'm right, maybe I'm wrong,
Maybe I'm lost or maybe belong,
Maybe I'll have to learn how to choose,
Because maybe I'm not prepared to lose!

TIME

I don't find any comfort within the hands of time,
That's what they said when life broke this heart of mine,
"Time will heal" they told me, it seems that I still wait,
Whoever said those words made a huge mistake!

How can I accept what I still cannot believe?
How can I move on if your memory never leaves?
How do I find answers when the questions linger on?
How can I make sense of the reason you are gone?

My life is like a movie, that time seems so surreal,
Someone hit the pause button for to this day I feel,
I'm back in that moment for my memories are raw,
Another missing piece of my own jigsaw.

I didn't want to lose you but I didn't have a choice,
I begged God to leave you but He didn't hear my voice,
I bargained every day that somehow He'd agree,
I couldn't live without you, I'd rather Him take me.

I long to find the comfort in the promises they make,
Instead this "time" they speak of only ever takes,
The peace from deep inside for it breaks my heart in two,
Time doesn't heal the pain, it just follows me through.

Angela McCrimmon

ANXIETY

"You're your own worst enemy!" I often hear that said,
Well you should try a day living in my head!
I over-think everything that you might ever say,
And when tomorrow comes I'll still be thinking of today.

I'll be watching you when you think you're watching me,
I will see much more than you could ever see,
I'll analyse each detail just to make sure I'm correct,
I'll tell you what you're thinking when you haven't said it yet.

I'll question your sincerity to make sure it is true,
I won't let it show I'm one step ahead of you,
I'll query your intentions and I won't let it rest,
I'm quite sure that I know my own prophecy is best.

We've had a lovely day and very pleasant night,
I'll wave you off goodbye and I'll know that I am right,
I'll think of conversations when I'm lying in my bed,
I cannot get to sleep so I'll think some more instead.

I'll think about the future, the present and the past,
I'll break down every word of conversation we had last,
I guarantee I'll find a word in every line,
The words that confirm we aren't really fine.

I think you need to realise for it's only fair you see,
You have got your work cut out if you do care for me,
Be patient when I drive you to such great and deep despair,
Think of how it feels for me....for I am living there!

I ADMIT

I have to admit that it hurt to hear,
The things you would sometimes say,
Maybe you said them out of fear?
Or maybe that's just a cliche.

I have to admit I didn't understand,
Why you just couldn't see,
Why wouldn't you hold my hand?
Until my mind could break free.

I have to admit I could feel it inside,
An anger burning within,
You made it clear you had to hide,
Me...too ashamed of my skin.

I have to admit I wanted to cry,
When I realised you'd always reject,
I'd sit alone and I'd wonder why?
I've not come up with an answer yet.

I have to admit that it hurt to know,
You really just did not care,
Lost, you left me nowhere to go,
I needed you, you weren't there.

I have to admit that I've left you behind,
Forgiveness is the reason I choose,
I realise acceptance you'll never find,
Because you've never walked in my shoes.

Angela McCrimmon

DEAR MEDICATION,

I can't remember my life without you,
I can't imagine it ever again,
You don't always do what you promise to,
But sometimes you help ease the pain.
You always fill me with such hope,
You're very deceptive that way,
It's like you had heard the words I spoke,
And you knew the right things to say.
You make promises you cannot keep,
Often you go unexplained,
Then occasionally a few of you meet,
And things are never the same.
I feel like you almost mix and match,
Give one hand, take back with the other,
You do your best to help me detach,
No intention to help me recover.
You visit me morning, noon and night,
Terrified I miss one dose,
Often I feel like one day I might,
Empty, discard, and dispose.
I guess I know that deep down inside,
That would be an expensive mistake,
I've been there before, pushed you aside,
So my sanity you chose to take.
You told me you'd help my anxiety ease,
You would lift my mood from the ground,
You would fill my mind with a gentle peace,
Paranoia not dancing around.
Over the years I admit it's true,
I would jump to your defence,
Then realise the problem was actually you,
You'd fooled me at what expense?
I have ordered a few of you just to go,
Walk away and don't come back,
Others I guess it's true I know,
Essential to keep me on track.
I don't hate you now for we're learning to live,
In harmony with each other,
Promises broken I will forgive,
For you DO want to help me recover!

SAYING GOODBYE

I remember the day that they stopped the clock,
The day they told me your time had been bought,
"We'll make him comfortable"...those dreaded words,
If there's a "comfortable" way to die it's absurd!

I'd armed myself with so many books,
Praying somehow they had overlooked,
Determined that I would find you a cure,
They'd made a mistake, of that I was sure.

Your diagnosis had stopped my heart,
You were far too young, when did it start?
Seeking answers with no explanation,
Only explaining your life expectation.

I could sense their pity when they came in the room,
Nurses would say "we'll be back in soon,"
I wanted to tell them I knew all along,
That this was the point where I had to be strong.

Each nurse and Dr had a different tone,
Individual "styles" of care they had shown,
The best by far whilst always complying,
Were the ones who didn't remind us you're dying.

You just wanted to chat about the football game,
How was the weekend? Was the "Nightlife" the same?
Was there anything good on the television?
Quick turn the channel if it's Eurovision!

(Cont'd)

(Cont'd)

We talked a lot, it was so surreal,
All you cared was how I'd feel,
"I'm going to send someone special to you,"
Only thinking of what I would do.

It didn't take long until your body grew weak,
Our eyes were the only way we could speak,
They gave us our space, they showed such respect,
They knew it was over though you hadn't gone yet.

I'll always remember the nurses there,
For all of their true compassion and care,
Please try to remember what they are relying,
Is on you to treat them like they are not dying.

CALM AND IN CONTROL

I know this feeling, the one that makes me squirm,
The thought alone makes my heart race,
The emotions it seems no facts can overturn,
The never ending conflict that I face.

The moment that makes me stop and hold my breath,
The temperature within my body rise,
I walk a fine line between my life and my death,
Of living by the truth and not by lies.

If I feel any judgement, deserved or unfound,
Anxiety starts to overwhelm,
Screaming in my head yet I cannot hear a sound,
My common-sense is in another realm.

I ask another question before giving it a chance,
I add to the dilemma even more,
Living on the edge, forever in a dance,
With one foot in and one foot out the door.

I live in constant danger for I catastrophise,
I tend to see the bad before the good,
The person I refuse to ever sympathise,
Is with myself, the one I really should.

For now I'm in control and I need to hold it tight,
For in a moment that control could go,
It's my responsibility to stand up here and fight,
And I'm damn sure I am going to let it show!

Angela McCrimmon

THANKFUL DREAD

I hate that feeling when I open my eyes,
I hold my breath in dread,
Will today be a morning to rise?
Or will I just stay in my bed?

I make my plans in hope that I,
Will be able to follow them through,
I pray to God that I can comply,
In all that I want to do.

My fight is just one day at a time,
Sometimes good, sometimes bad,
I tell myself I'm going to be fine,
If ever I find myself sad.

I'm not quite sure until I wake,
Just how my day's going to go,
I hope so much the plans I make,
Will allow my mind to slow.

I guess the truth is I should try,
To look at things this way,
Some people had to say goodbye,
And will not wake up today.

So every time I open my eyes,
I will thank the Lord up above,
For giving me another day to rise,
To be with all the people I love.

BREATHE

I need to take a moment to simply stop and breathe,
I need to tell these thoughts to get right up and leave,
They are no longer welcome, no longer have a place,
I need them out my life and I need them out my space.

It seems as if they always try to creep back in,
They know my insecurities that I hold within,
They know just when to get me and what they need to do,
But this time I will tell them "I'm one step ahead of you!"

I know what I am feeling and I know I'll be okay,
I know that they will listen when I send them on their way,
For finally they understand that I am in control,
They might try to break me but I will keep me whole.

I used to always panic thinking "here we go again,"
I have to just remember that this is now not then,
And where I'm standing now is many miles away,
From where I was standing right back in yesterday.

2
Don't Judge
A Book By Its Cover

"I don't want you to save me I want you to stand by my side as I save myself" — Sushil Singh, The Flexible Enterprise

I learned quickly that in the Mental Health System my own thoughts and opinions were inconsequential. Eventually this realisation brought with it an intensity of frustration as the words were there, I just wasn't given the chance or respect to share them. Assumptions were made, treatment unfair, and most of all I was scared into silence. Terrified, frustrated, angry and very, very misunderstood. I don't fit neatly in a box but unfortunately I found myself in one that by their theories I would never climb out.

DON'T JUDGE A BOOK BY ITS COVER

I see you sit in judgement, I hear it loud and clear,
I sense your criticism because it's what I fear,
If you could only see, if you'd only understand,
Maybe then you'd know why I am the way I am.

I can see you watching me yet you're blind in many ways,
You base your explanation on what a textbook says,
You draw up your conclusion and for all the time it took,
You seem to miss the point.....that I am not a book!

I feel like you won't help me and it seems that you don't try,
Just take the time to ask me and I will tell you why,
Please just take a moment, please give me space to breathe,
All I ask is for your patience, give me time to grieve.

I'm not so complicated and if only you could see,
I'm stronger than you think, please just look at me,
Please just stand beside me instead of write me off,
"No discrimination" is the part that you forgot!

I'm not a diagnosis, I'm not part of your game,
I hoped that you might help me unpack some of the pain,
I prayed you'd understand the things I hold within,
Please don't judge my story by the chapter you walked in!

Angela McCrimmon

I FEEL...

I feel so frightened, I'm scared beyond compare,
You treat me as if you don't see me standing there.
I feel so forgotten, it seems you all dismiss,
It's like you don't acknowledge that something is amiss.
I feel so confused, nothing's making sense,
Why are you bewildered when the doubt is so intense?
I feel so depressed yet you just don't believe,
I need your reassurance but you turn around and leave.
I feel so detached, my head just disconnects,
It's clear you are despondent and show me no respect.
I feel so aware, my sensitivity is acute,
Your ignorance is clear when you don't take time to look.
I feel so hurt when you break my heart in two,
Put yourself in my place, what if this were you?
I feel so afraid, too ashamed to ask for help,
You do not seem to see how much I help myself.
I feel very sad, I'm so misunderstood,
You don't treat or care for me the way I know you should.
If I could ask one thing of you, I'd ask you if you're able,
Please try to treat my symptoms.....and not just my label.

PERFECTLY PARANOID

Sometimes I feel like there's no point in trying,
I try to explain but they think I am lying,
I'm wasting their time and they make that so clear,
I start to think what's the point in being here?

I came here to beg them to help me somehow,
Each time sent away so each time I'd vow,
Never to ask them ever again,
Because no matter what it's always the same.

I've a million examples but one I will share,
I nervously approached a nurse standing there,
I quietly said "Could I have medication?"
She stood there demanding an explanation.

I'd woken so anxious and troubled that day,
When I tried to express this all she could say,
"Hmph, well you don't look anxious to me,"
She turned and left not willing to see.

I was shocked because I'd never asked before,
I headed towards my bedroom door,
"Not anxious" and so medication foregone,
Well excuse me while I go put my anxious face on!

They say that my paranoia's unfound,
I know it's not but I don't make a sound,
What's the point in trying to say...
"It's you that's made me feel this way!!"

I'M NOT A VICTIM

I'm not a victim....I fight to survive,
I'm not a victim...Look, I'm alive!
I'm not a victim....Why do you say?
I'm not a victim....Get out of my way!
I'm not a victim....But sometimes I fall,
I'm not a victim....You don't know me at all!
I'm not a victim....You don't see me cry,
I'm not a victim.... I rarely ask "WHY??"
I'm not a victim....I keep fighting on,
I'm not a victim....My hope's never gone!
I'm not a victim....You don't seem to see,
I'm not a victim.... I fight to be free!
I'm not a victim....Most people can't tell,
I'm not a victim...I'll get out of this hell!
I'm not a victim....I just make mistakes,
I'm not a victim....But sometimes I break!
I'm not a victim....I'll never give up,
I'm not a victim....so shut the hell up!

TABLES TURNED

You might be watching me, but I am watching you,
You think that you're listening but I am hearing you,
You read my body language but I read yours loud and clear,
You're present in the room but your mind it isn't here.

Each clicking of your pen, each tapping of your foot,
I wonder what you scribble in your "official" looking book?
I wonder what you think you had the right to claim?
To write it in my notes and to which you ascertain.

You change the medication, try a different dose,
I cling in desperation to overcome the lows,
I know what you are saying and it makes no sense at all,
You tick another box and try to put me in them all.

I observe what you are wearing, colourful or grey,
I hear the roaring volume in the things you do not say,
I look at you directly to look you in the eye,
I'm pleading for the truth, please not another lie.

I'm sorry I'm boring you, that you don't have the time,
You roll your eyes so tiresome and say the words "It's fine,"
Ironically you mean those words from you to me,
I'm speaking them right back because "It's fine" will never be.

I get up from the chair and walk towards the door,
Each step a little hesitant than the one before,
I glance back in hope that you'll glance at me too,
In silent desperation that you're going to help me through.

I guess the lesson learned is the one you taught so well,
Sometimes my story is the one I cannot tell,
So when you're watching me, remember this is true,
If you look a little closer you will see I'm watching you.

Angela McCrimmon

WHAT WE NEED

I stand here today but I don't just stand for me,
Finally a voice to somehow make you see,
So much unspoken for you don't understand,
Terrified for sometimes our life is in your hands.

Self- advocacy but sometimes we can't communicate,
Knowing one day that it's going to be too late,
Your judgement unfair for you just don't comprehend,
We need you to step in when on you we must depend.

We try our best to tell you and we try to just explain,
Devastated when your response always the same,
"Take responsibility" we try our best to do,
You don't seem to see this and it breaks our heart in two.

We fight a daily battle that you could never know,
Please help keep us safe, don't tell us to go,
There shouldn't be such conflict between you and I,
We need to work together, please don't make us cry.

THERAPY

I'm sitting over here, you're sitting over there,
I always know my "allocated" chair,
I have to admit I am sceptical though,
I do my best to never let it show.

I cringe when I remember the things I've said,
The email I wrote lying in my bed,
I wasn't sure where the madness would end,
I opened my heart then hit the key "send."

Can you read my thoughts or am I hiding it well?
Do you realise there's a story I cannot tell?
I tell you so much but hold something back,
I don't know why, maybe trust I lack?

Your expression can surely communicate,
Not sure if you realise the chance that I take?
The chance to ask what I've always known,
The answers confirmed to the questions thrown.

A lifetime of learning to dissociate,
Why would I want to be somewhere I hate?
To me it makes such perfect sense,
Disconnect from the world but at what expense?

The time is up and relief overflows,
Return to the person that nobody knows,
I retreat to my world to contemplate,
Can you save my life or is it just too late?

Angela McCrimmon

DR FOR A DAY

If I could be the Dr for maybe just a day,
Maybe then you'd see and understand?
How much you hear in the words I do not say,
And how much your life is in my hands.

I'd tell you what I think then do my best to look,
Pretending that I truly contemplate,
I'd maybe take a moment to check my little book,
Then rush you out the door, I'm running late.

I'd feel exasperated and I would let it show,
I'd cut your sentence off before you end,
I'd always make it clear that I already know,
How this situation's going to end.

I wonder how you'd feel if you never had the chance?
To say or speak whatever's on your mind,
Would you finally switch off, drift off in a trance?
The "I don't care...I've had enough" kind.

I'd tell you I have met so many just like you,
I've treated so many of your "kind,"
"Trust me" I'd say and I'd expect you to,
For I am the commander of your mind.

I'd tell you that I'm weary, I've heard it all before,
You've said this to me time after time,
I'm present in the room but I'm looking at the door,
I tell you "Oh, it's going to be just fine."

The problem that we have is you just don't trust,
A single word that I am going to say,
So with this in mind I guess I really must,
Accept I won't be Dr for the day.

BACK TO THE FUTURE

The hospital walls already knew my name,
Although they hadn't seen me for a while,
They were still here, everything the same,
It's me who has walked on another mile.

Where once I found comfort I now felt fear,
The nausea settled deep inside,
Gone were the days I longed to be here,
A respite from the world where I could hide.

I heard the desperation of people coming in,
Emotionally driven to despair,
I sympathised and felt their turmoil within,
For it wasn't long ago I too was there.

Nurses rushed by as if they hadn't seen me there,
Others shared a smile to say hello,
An awkward understanding they weren't there to care,
For me their care had come and had to go.

I kept one eye on the clock for I knew the routine,
The routine that had always held such fear,
I knew all the "signals" and what each one would mean,
Like when they say the words, "Step over here."

On one side I could see patients crying out,
The other side could barely stay awake,
Some would recoil while others chose to shout,
But most of them they chose to medicate.

Everyone was anxious but some more than most,
Some patients walked from room to room,
A look of disturb as if they'd seen a ghost,
Or else that they would see one very soon.

Something struck me hard as I realised it was true,
Where once there felt no unity just divide,
I'd always felt this ward was "me against you,"
Now I realise we were all on the same side.

Angela McCrimmon

RIDDLE....DISCHARGE GUARANTEED

You always have me even when you don't,
I will tell them you will even when you won't,
I'm a reminder whenever you have forgot,
I'll tell them you can even when you cannot.

Never more in danger than whenever I'm safe,
Never less hopeful than when I give you faith,
A message conveyed in all that I do,
I'm nearby to show you are thinking it through.

Such volume in silence with a deafening tone,
Safety in numbers when standing alone,
Such clarity with an ironic view,
I'll make sure everyone else sees me too.

I'll ensure you're dismissed in your desperate plea,
I'll push you aside and say "Look at me!"
I'll step forward whenever you try to step back,
I'm "Capacity" and it is I, of which you do not lack!

EXPRESSIONS

Why do people say "Pull your socks up??"
A ridiculous expression to say,
I want to tell them to just "shut up,"
So I know I must walk away.

They make it sound easy like it's my choice,
If only I had their vision,
Maybe then they would hear my voice?
It's a disorder, not a decision!

They tell me I just need to "get a grip,"
I can feel my anger inside,
Upset by their insensitive quip,
My emotions I have to hide.

I hear them say "She's a Drama Queen,"
I know what they're trying to say,
I remain so calm but inside I scream,
The leading role in my very own play!

Maybe one day my socks will be high,
And maybe I WILL have a choice,
I'll "get a grip" and I'll say goodbye,
To my "Drama Queen" overused voice!

Angela McCrimmon

SURVIVOR

Did you really think I wouldn't fight back?
Did you really believe I would stay?
You underestimated the fact,
I'll fight 'til my dying day!

Fall down 7 times, Get up 8,
Determined I know that I am,
I'm afraid I'm not prepared to wait,
When you say I can't I say can!

I almost laugh when I think that you could,
Misjudge me to this extent,
I think you've confused me for someone who would,
Believe all the words that you meant!

I have more courage than you'll ever know,
Resilient is my middle name,
I'm aware that sometimes it doesn't show,
So I guess I would think the same.

I'm writing this poem to get the words out,
The words that run through my head,
I don't want to scream and you won't hear me shout,
So I'm silently fighting instead.

I know that I may take longer than some,
I've taken the long way too,
The game is over for the fight is won,
I'm just sorry it was me against you.

PSYCHITRIST APPOINTMENT

When you meet me next what will you see?
Will you look at the illness or will you look at me?
Will you be surprised at the progress I've made?
How the "Borderline traits" continue to fade.

Will my remarkable progress start to confuse?
The diagnostic criteria used,
Am I really quite so cut and so clear?
May I get out my box and stand over here?

I hope you will see that the medication,
Is perfect with not a sign of sedation,
These days feel like it's no effort to make,
Since the increased dose you allowed me to take.

Maybe you'll be the Dr who can?
Finally see the person I am,
To harm myself I do not require,
Recovery is all I've ever desired.

12 months and consistently well,
Through these months I've a story to tell,
"Complex" may be my middle name,
I tried to tell you it wasn't the same.

I think we know that I have my thoughts,
Of all that I am and of all I'm not,
I've always felt misunderstood,
They saw the bad and missed the good.

I've no idea what conclusion you'll find?
Maybe I am just one of a kind?
"Dual diagnosis" or maybe just one?
I live for the day my diagnosis is "None."

Angela McCrimmon

FINISH LINE

I know you have your theory of the way that I should be,
You see a diagnosis when you should be seeing me,
I wish that I could tell you all the reasons you are wrong,
But I am not the Dr so my thoughts do not belong.

You had me all worked out from the research that you do,
What you seem to miss is that I research things too,
I research in my hope that the answers I will find,
For you have given up and are leaving me behind.

The notes that you've read lately are really quite unfair,
If you'd look beyond the lies you would find me there,
Instead you look right through me like I'm not in the room,
I bow my head in silence for I see that you assume.

It seems you misinterpret all the things I say and do,
You have your understanding but I have my own too,
I've done a lot of searching and I know deep in my heart,
I will cross the finish line before you even start.

MIRROR IMAGE

You start the conversation in that old familiar tone,
It seems the only voice that you're hearing is your own,
It seems you are surprised when you see I've thought it through,
Articulated answers are the only kind I do.

You tell me that it's just another symptom you expect,
You tell me that the medication isn't working yet,
What you do not realise, what you don't seem to see,
I'm the expert in the room when it comes to me.

I have my education and I'm sure that you can tell,
I'm not what you expected for you thought you knew me well,
You'd seen my "type" before but you didn't think that I,
Would stand up for myself or even look you in the eye.

I'm not afraid to tell you in the most "appropriate" way,
I don't need to scream for you to hear just what I say,
The only thing I ask is that you do understand,
My opinion counts as well, not just what you demand.

When you look in the mirror I hope that you might see,
The reflection staring back at you is similar to me,
We're really not that different and the point I want to make,
You give me your advice but it's your own you need to take!

Angela McCrimmon

INTRODUCTIONS

You seem a bit confused and not sure what you see,
I think that you're still trying to work me out,
Let me take a moment to just introduce "me,"
We missed that introduction there's no doubt!

You seem a bit bewildered and a little perplexed,
That's okay for I can understand,
For so long you weren't sure what I'd do next,
Yet here I am so grounded on dry land.

You seem a bit surprised and I know you question why,
What has changed to make me feel so well?
The answer is simple...the new dose you let me try,
Although I know that only time will tell.

You seem a bit unsure and a little sceptical,
This wasn't what you thought that you would see,
You see my behaviour is quite respectable,
I'm maybe not the case you thought I'd be.

You seem to have some faith like you're starting to believe,
I'm not someone who wants to be unwell,
I'll fight to hell and back to find my own reprieve,
And I will have a story I can tell.

We've had our introductions and I'm glad that you've met,
The side of me the others didn't see,
I hope that we are finding a true mutual respect,
I'm so much more than you thought I would be.

BACK TO SCHOOL

You're listening but I'm thinking "Why are you here?!"
It's clear you are in the wrong job,
Maybe this wasn't your chosen career?
It's just the only one you have got!

It's ironic I guess because I know it's true,
We might well be slightly insane,
It doesn't mean that we cannot see through,
Just where you are placing the blame.

Where's your compassion when you cut us off?
Where is your care and concern?
The illness we fight, it seems like you scoff,
We see you have so much to learn.

We have our good days, we have our bad,
And some days don't happen at all,
Please understand when we're feeling sad,
Please help us up when we fall.

We want to talk "to" but you're talking "at,"
We don't have a chance to respond,
It's clear you've made the assumption that,
You are right and we're always wrong.

"First Do No Harm," that's what you said,
Do you remember the oath you took?
Are you aware just where we go in our head?
No, because you don't even look!

I speak for most when I simply say,
You need to go back to school,
Because maybe it seems at the end of the day,
We're the ones you will never fool.

Angela McCrimmon

UNSPOKEN WORDS

So much I keep inside for fear you won't believe,
That thought is terrifying on its own,
I'm scared you would think that I'd set out to deceive,
So I'll walk this winding path all alone.

Sometimes I'm confused and I cannot understand,
So many thoughts race around my head,
Thoughts of expectations that you might demand,
Such fear that I will disappoint instead.

You look at me with eyes that speak a million words,
They have a language of their very own,
You look at me as if I'm really quite absurd,
Through not one single word I hear the tone.

I know you're the "expert" but I'm an expert too,
After all the "subject" now is me,
If you do not mind, if it's okay with you,
I'd like to consult with myself to see.

It seems no consultation or how much I confer,
Will change the conclusion you have found,
If you'd consider NOT using my notes to refer,
You'd see my silence really is profound.

A MASK

I wonder if they ever take the time to think?
I wonder if they truly understand?
We turn to them for help when we are on the brink,
Do they realise that our life is in their hands?

Some use the approach of "Cruel to be kind,"
All that ever does is break my heart,
I feel insanity is racing through my mind,
I see the end before I even start.

I'm caught up in the madness and I want to shout,
"Please Help Me" for I am feeling scared,
I feel deep inside that my strength is running out,
So familiar yet I'm always unprepared.

I wonder if they ever stop to realise?
That we don't all fit neatly in a box,
The "labels" they attach are all that I despise,
I'm many things but textbook I am not!

I guess I'll never know for I will never ask,
I don't think they would answer anyway,
Would I find a human if I saw beyond their mask?
I'm guessing in this box I'll have to stay.

Angela McCrimmon

ALL I ASK

If I could find the words I know what I would say,
My vocabulary has become my very stage,
I'll never stop believing that there will come a day,
When this chapter will be closed, I'll turn the page.

You only hear one voice and it's sad for me to see,
The only language that you seem to hear,
The words that are coming from you and not from me,
Your conception of the truth is what I fear.

You see the behaviour and you don't look beyond,
The message that is burning in my soul,
Are you really so naive to think it's coming from,
A place of hate for all life ever stole?

I know that I'm not "bad" and I don't hate myself,
So please allow this theory to dispel,
I simply left my feelings sitting on the shelf,
They're trying to escape and I'm in hell.

You see no self-esteem yet I know it is true,
I know that I have so much I can give,
How can I express these words from me to you?
I long for nothing more than but to live.

You think you know my story so you put me in box,
You make me into everything I fear,
I hope that maybe one day you'll see my real thoughts,
All I ask is that you don't leave me here.

YOU TOLD ME

You told me I had to stand up and find my voice,
You told me that my actions would always be my choice,
You told me my "capacity" would always see me through,
I don't think I am looking at the same person as you.

You told me I would live forever in a storm,
No sooner up then down, nowhere to belong,
You put me in box but I refused to stay,
For fear you'd see an "outburst" so too afraid to say.

I tried to so hard to tell you but I just could not express,
You wouldn't see the difference, couldn't see how more is less,
I tried so hard to scream for I needed you to save,
God knows how I'm alive and not lying in a grave!

You told me I'm intelligent and of that I do agree,
That was half my problem, why could you not see?
I begged you to just realise the danger I was in,
My "intelligence" was the reason my death wish would win.

You told me it was time to realise all the pain,
I was causing my loved ones time and time again,
If you could only see how that really broke my heart,
I already felt such guilt for tearing them apart.

You told me you would help me but it would take some time,
A long road to recovery, to claw back this life of mine,
It seems you all were wrong for I hadn't far to go,
Just one thing left to say… "I guess I told you so."

Angela McCrimmon

APPRENTICESHIP

I've done my "apprenticeship" that's for sure,
Years of experience to date,
So much heartache that I have endured,
Often thinking it could be too late.

Too late to turn my life around,
I'd been down this road before,
Always pushed back on the ground,
Each time I came back for more.

So many missed the strength inside,
Evidently I stand here today,
Not many thought I'd even survive,
Even less I'd have something to say.

I guess that's the thing when you lose your voice,
It's not that the words aren't there,
You just accept you don't have a choice,
Message received they don't care.

My voice may have silenced but my eyes could see,
My ears can hear crystal clear,
My own opinion longed to break free,
But I knew that it had no place here.

I knew that any attempt to speak out,
Would just tick another box,
I wanted to scream and I wanted to shout,
I stayed silent for I knew I dare not.

You make it clear that it's all in my head,
What a ridiculous statement it seems,
Subliminal message that maybe instead,
They'd believe me if my pain could be seen.

An invisible wound has a story to tell,
Just one page or maybe a book,
My "apprenticeship" has taught me well,
So could yours...if you took time to look!!

YOU SAY...

You say you want to help me to heal this heart of mine,
Yet when I start to talk you say you haven't time,
It was hard to find the courage to open up my mouth,
Then you stopped me in my tracks before the words came out.

You say you think I'm ready and it's time for me to leave,
I pause in hesitation for it's clear that you believe,
You ask in such a way that it's evident to me,
Your own opinion is the only one you see.

You say I'm being "irrational" then tell me it makes sense,
Forgive me if I doubt and I jump to my defence,
It's just the diagnosis you associate such shame,
Just for the record, do you even know my name??

You say I'm being dramatic and it's simply what I do,
May I excuse myself so I can prepare for Act 2?
I can assure you that if I had the skills to grace the stage,
I wouldn't still be learning my lines from the last page.

You say that I'll grow out of this, one day I won't "act out,"
If it wasn't for maturity I know that I'd scream out,
I've always had more wisdom, wise beyond my years,
You seem to miss that point when you're looking at my tears.

You say so many things to me but all I hear is noise,
You tell me that you're listening but I only hear your voice,
Maybe I should tell you now and get it out the way,
I'm actually not listening to a single word you say!!

Angela McCrimmon

IT HURTS

It hurts to know you hear me but you don't understand,
To realise you don't know me, you don't know who I am,
To realise you misread all the signs you have been shown,
You're standing right beside me and yet I feel alone.

It hurts to know you judge me, unjustified it's true,
Your eyes may be closed but mine are watching you,
Your eyes may be glazed but mine are crystal clear,
You're present in the room but your mind it isn't here.

It hurts to know you cannot and you will not even try,
Not interested you are quite content to walk on by,
Not interested and it seems so evident to me,
You are quite despondent to however I might be.

It hurts to know I'm hurting and you really do not care,
You say you're "unavailable" but I see you standing there,
You say you'll call me back but I know you never will,
Instead you try to silence me, prescribe another pill.

It hurts to know and realise that I'm in this fight alone,
To understand the meaning of the care you haven't shown,
To understand the person I am turning out to be,
Is thanks to myself, and thanks to only me!

CONVERSATION

If I could ask one question I know what it would be,
There's just one thing I'd really like to ask,
When you look in my direction tell me what you see,
My illness...myself...or just a mask?

I'd ask you why you think all the things you do?
I'd ask you what makes you seem so sure?
Maybe you are looking at a patient you once knew?
Why do you assume my thoughts obscure?

If we had a conversation would you let me talk?
Would my opinion count for anything?
No other Dr has so maybe you would not,
My own input would you let me bring?

If I could be the Dr for maybe just a day,
And you were my patient in that chair,
How would you feel about all the things I say?
I wonder if you'd feel they were unfair?

I know what you are thinking, you'd say that it depends,
You'd check if my philosophy was true,
Maybe you'd receive the message that it sends?
The message I am hearing now from you.

I wonder if you've stopped, maybe just to pause?
To realise I may not be cut or clear,
You've taken so much time pointing out my flaws,
It seems you've missed the person standing here.

I guess if I am honest I know that it is true,
These answers never will exist,
You don't believe me and I don't believe you,
Another conversation dismissed.

Angela McCrimmon

YOUR TYPE

You ask me how I am so I smile and say "Okay,"
It seems the easy answer for I know what you would say,
What's the point in telling you what you don't want to hear?
Risking your rejection, the one thing that I fear.

We all have a story, only some we read aloud,
Other chapters we hold back for we are very proud,
There are many just like you I've written in my book,
The ones who didn't even care enough to look.

I'm standing here alone, you should be by my side,
They tell me I should open up, you make me want to hide,
You show me no emotion so I shut mine down too,
You tell me that you care but I can tell that isn't true.

You say I'm lost in music and that life it will not wait,
My music's healing pain that no pill could medicate,
I turned down the volume so I could hear you speak,
You didn't....so in music, that comfort I do seek.

I know I'm just a number that I'm not even a name,
I've met your type before and your "type" are all the same,
So when you ask me how I am, I'll smile and say "Okay,"
What's the point in answering, you don't care anyway?

MISUNDERSTOOD

I tried so hard to tell them but they just couldn't see,
The person they were looking at really wasn't me,
The person I was begging them to somehow help me find,
The person that I knew I was before I'd lost my mind!

It's like they seen the illness and they couldn't look beyond,
They had their own assumptions of the way I would respond,
They had their own opinion on behaviour I displayed,
They didn't understand me and it left me so afraid.

I knew how hard I'd fallen, I knew I was unwell,
I tried to make them see but it seems they couldn't tell,
Now I'm getting better and I'm getting on my feet,
I hope that they are seeing this every time we meet.

I hope they can see this other person standing here,
I hope they can see that my mind is sharp and clear,
I can only pray that they truly comprehend,
The difference in me now compared to way back then.

I guess I'll never ask and they might never tell,
I pray they're taking note of the "real me" when I'm well,
That way I'd rest assured that next time they would see,
Whether they are dealing with the illness or with me.

Angela McCrimmon

CONFLICT

I don't fit the "mould" I know that it's true,
No DSM diagnosis for me,
I don't respond the way you want me to,
Nothing makes sense so you see.
No textbook case to diagnose,
And certainly no pill to fix,
I can't help being this way I should know,
It's NOT my mind playing tricks!
For any solution I'm desperate to find,
I've walked to hell and beyond,
You're not the one who lives in my mind,
Always knowing I'm right being told wrong.
"The maximum dose" just does not apply,
The "combination" just doesn't go,
From pure frustration I want to cry,
"It's my body.... my head..... I should know!!"
Dismissed once again I hold back the tears,
Why can you just not see?
The one and only thing that I fear,
Is the conflict between you and me.

STAND UP

They say we should stand for something so I'm standing for this,
A voice for the broken, to ensure we're not dismissed,
An example of the fact that you should not discriminate,
We don't dislike ourselves, it's the illness that we hate.

We don't want to wear a label to help you to define,
Whatever mental illness takes over our minds,
To you a diagnosis, to us it's a compromise,
Our place within society and all that it implies.

We are all individuals yet quite often just the same,
We get off the rollercoaster then we get back on again,
We have much more wisdom and the credit we are due,
That's why I'm going to fight to try and educate you.

We don't want "attention"...it's "understanding" that we seek,
All we want is you to listen when we find the strength to speak,
It's important you're aware that our opinion counts too,
It's crucial you realise what your ignorance can do.

I won't drown anymore in the sadness or the shame,
If I get knocked down I'll get up and fight again,
I'll fight for the many damaged injured souls,
And for all the self- respect that our mental illness stole.

Most of all I'll stand up for what I truly do believe,
The things so clear to me yet what you do not perceive,
The things that I have learned as I've travelled on my way,
I'll stand up for the reasons I am standing here today.

3

First Do No Harm

Having so much to say and no chance to say it meant a huge amount of frustration. As a child I functioned very highly at the expense of severe internal anxiety....around the age of 14 I discovered a way to cope with this. Self-Harm. Successfully hidden for over 10 years which dispels the theory that self-harm is attention seeking. I simply hurt on the outside because I hurt on the inside.

THE EMERGENCY ROOM

I don't want to go because you always make it clear,
"Attention seeking behaviour" is the reason I am here,
What you do not see is how hard I've truly tried,
To treat it on my own, for fear a label is applied.

The last time this happened you said I'm wasting time,
No insight whatsoever inside this head of mine,
You...they...them...none of you have a clue,
No gentle compassion when you ask "What's wrong with you?"

It went from my Nurse who could very clearly see,
I needed desperate help or who knows where I'd be,
She doesn't pass her judgement for it isn't hers to give,
She only cares for me.....she cares that I should live.

You tell me to seek help but what you don't understand,
It's you that fuels my fear from the answers you demand,
The answers that are written in each wound that you neglect,
You're holding my heart yet you haven't found yours yet.

Angela McCrimmon

WHO I AM

I try so hard not to self- harm,
It is what I do but it's not who I am,
It is what you see upon the outside,
Yet you miss what it says about what I hide.

You miss that my heart is breaking in two,
I know you think it's just what I do,
I know that it's clear you always dismiss,
How on earth did it ever come to this?

Responsibility I do not diminish,
I try to say but you don't let me finish,
I try to tell you I know I'm to blame,
It's just my way to handle the pain.

To punish myself you seem to assume,
I see your stare from across the room,
You all seem to talk as if I'm not there,
Your judgement unfound and simply unfair.

I'll never give up on this battle I fight,
For I pray that things will be alright,
I try so hard not to self-harm,
It is what I do but it's not who I am.

MY PLACE OF SAFETY

Lost in a world that no-one can see,
But I'm happy and safe right here,
It's the one and only place I can be...
Myself with nothing to fear.

I can hold my pen, allow it to move,
Wherever it wants to go,
It's for my eyes only, nothing to prove,
Not another soul will I show.

I'm secure and not at risk for I know,
My feelings are not burning up,
I can be who I am, not put on a show,
While inside my emotions erupt.

There's no-one to say they don't believe,
A word that I'm trying to say,
There's no-one there to wrongly perceive,
It's helping me get through the day.

I don't hurt here, no need for harm,
My pen and paper provide,
The canvas I need to say who I am,
And all that I'm feeling inside.

Angela McCrimmon

ALIVE

If I could find a way to make you understand,
I'd ask you to look harder and see beyond the harm,
I wish that I could find a way to make you see,
The scars you are looking at are now a part of me.

I cannot change the past but I will not regret,
I truly do believe my story isn't over yet,
I truly do believe that for all that I've been through,
I am going to fight to try and educate you.

The wounds that I inflicted helped me to survive,
Self- harm is the reason I know I'm still alive,
When life overwhelmed me and I just couldn't cope,
The pain carried me through and I held onto hope.

I didn't harm to hurt, I thought my harm would heal,
So ashamed of my secret I knew I must conceal,
Each wound and all the damage you wouldn't understand,
My self- harm was there when you let go of my hand.

You make your own assumptions but what you overlook,
Is the fact I'm still standing and all the strength it took,
To survive in a world where I didn't want to be,
The reason I am living are the scars that you can see.

SCARED

I can feel things slipping away from me,
I'm trying to hide so they can't see,
The anxiety's gripping deep inside,
I'm doing my best to try and hide.
"I don't feel well," what they don't know,
Is it's in my head but I can't show,
These days there's so much expectation,
I've created my own situation.
Reaching heights I'd only dreamed,
My self-respect I had redeemed,
Opportunities fierce and fast,
Maybe it was too good to last?
Even my writing has all but dried,
My words had been my way to cry,
Instead I've kept them all locked in,
Emotions trapped and held within.
Each plan cancelled that I'd made,
Trust in myself begins to fade,
I'm not angry, I'm just so scared,
This feeling, I was so unprepared.
I'm not ready to face the world yet,
I'm going to try just step by step,
I can't relapse, I can't stay down,
From this I know I must rebound.
The thought to harm has crossed my mind,
I promised I'd left that all behind,
I'm learning it's never far from me,
Waiting in the wings for all to see.
I have to sort my head right out,
Remind my heart what life's about,
I've found these words, it's been so long,
Maybe everything's not so wrong.

Angela McCrimmon

BEHIND CLOSED DOORS

They tell you that you shouldn't judge unless you've stood there,
To criticise what you don't know is really quite unfair,
To assume that it's all their fault and something they would choose,
We wouldn't know the answer until we've walked in their shoes.

You do not know the demons that they try so hard to fight,
Or what's waiting for them when they close the door at night,
You say it's their own doing and that they should walk away,
Their shame and their terror is the reason that they stay.

We do not know their nightmare and be thankful that we don't,
The fear that determines if they will or if they won't,
Run for their life but where would they run to?
Until you have been there you don't know what you'd do.

So stop for a moment and just take time to breathe,
Don't assume the battle is their choice to ever leave,
You may not understand it but what you MUST understand,
They don't want your judgement, they only want your hand.

PLEASE HELP, NOT HURT

Another layer of sadness, another layer of shame,
I bring it on myself so I'm the one to blame,
I take responsibility although you think I don't,
You don't seem to see that, or maybe you just won't?

You're asking me questions but I don't want to talk,
I cannot find the answers, drowning in my thoughts,
Drowning in this madness for here we are again,
I dare not look at you for I know you think the same.

"So how did this happen?" the first Dr asks,
Repeated by the 2nd, 3rd, 4th and last,
I've tried to be polite but inside I scream,
"You already know!!" and we both know what I mean.

You call for the Psychiatrist but if you only knew,
There's absolutely nothing that they are going to do,
I've been here before and I know the story well,
They silence me each time so my story I don't tell.

I let them "tick their box" just like they do each time,
The little box that states "she's absolutely fine,"
The little box that says "please do not detain,"
I guess in their eyes they think I'll never change.

73

Angela McCrimmon

HOSPITALISATION

I try to take care of it all on my own,
I pray that this will remain unknown,
They have no idea the level of shame,
When they have to take care all over again.

There are some who make it very clear,
Disgust, I don't deserve to be here,
What they miss is that I feel the same,
I'm well aware I'm the one to blame.

They bring my meal, I don't want to eat,
I try to protest then admit defeat,
Extra calories they make me consume,
Sometimes watching, won't leave the room.

It appears that septicaemia set in,
Antibiotics are going to begin,
No time for a drip, straight in the vein,
The needle too deep in their haste causes pain.

Post- surgery needs attentive care,
To ensure the graft stays right there,
Sometimes left in a dressing so wet,
Always the same, they just seem to "forget."

"Ward Round" the part I hate the most,
Each morning the Drs stand in close,
The nurses "brief" on my progress,
Yet truly I feel they couldn't care less.

Sometimes I persevere with the pain,
It's too much effort to try to explain,
This pain I feel is not like before,
They wouldn't understand that less is more.

SELF-MEDICATION

I begged them to help but they turned me away,
I tried by myself but what could I say?
I failed and I started a new nightmare,
It felt like the only thing that was there.
It started off with what the Drs gave,
My life was in danger, I was trying to save,
I knew my own risk that they couldn't see,
If I didn't act fast I knew where I'd be!
I begged the Drs time and again,
Each time their answer would be the same,
I knew that soon it would be too late,
I saw no option but to "self-medicate."
The months went by, it was always the same,
Take another pill to escape the pain,
Take another tablet when I felt unsafe,
Struggling to function or even think straight.
"Tolerance" it seems it crept on in,
So scared of what I would do to my skin,
No other option but increase the dose,
Another secret that nobody knows.
Another secret I had to hide,
So much hidden, so deep inside,
The illness I have, this illness I curse,
My Self-Medication made everything worse.
Caught in a cycle I knew it must stop,
Enough was enough and I knew I must not,
Continue this madness but I didn't see,
Addiction crept in and took hold of me.
In horror I realised just what I'd done,
Knowing that this time I couldn't run,
Knowing I had to be honest and true,
It was the only way that I would pull through.

(cont'd)

(cont'd)

I won't say it's easy and I had to fight,
I kept the finish line in my sight,
So strong were my feelings to hurt and destroy,
Not sure how I'd ever again feel the joy.
Not sure how I'd cope without that pill,
I vowed then and there that somehow I will,
I realised the answers didn't lie there,
They lay within me and I had to go there.
This chapter is done and I turned the page,
So trapped but I escaped from that cage,
Lessons I learned and the answers I found,
I survived addiction but I almost drowned.

PAPER

I'm looking for some paper, I'm reaching for a pen,
I need to find it fast for if I don't that's when,
My thoughts will take right over leaving me behind,
Eating up my soul and tearing through my mind.

I know what will happen if I cannot let it out,
Of that there is no question, of this there is no doubt,
The fear hits me hard as I realise it is true,
There's only one way back or I know what I will do.

My heart's beating faster with the panic setting in,
The story will be over the moment it begins,
I've been here at least 100 times before,
I need to write it down then I need to write some more.

I wrote so many chapters on a place where I could see,
Each and every word staring back at me,
I wrote it on myself with a marker made of red,
If I can't find some paper there's a chance I will be dead.

Angela McCrimmon

A SPECIAL NURSE...LOUISE

My place of safety when I was scared,
One step ahead when unprepared,
The one who reached out with her hand,
Who took the time to understand.
Never the thought that I deceived,
They hurt my heart when disbelieved,
Never the one to pass me by,
A hug to hold me when I cried.
The one who heard my cry for help,
Tried to protect me from myself,
Assurance that I'd be okay,
She always knew the words to say.
Her soul destroyed when every time,
She clearly seen I wasn't fine,
She tried to make them hear my voice,
Knowing I didn't have a choice.
The one who said a silent prayer,
The only one who seemed to care,
The one who tried to take the knife,
The only one who saved my life.

OLD FRIENDS

You tried to drop by yesterday,
So sorry I wasn't home,
You left a note on my door to say,
I don't have to feel so alone.
I have to admit it's probably true,
Nobody understands,
Nobody "gets" me like you do,
You were always so close at hand.
Best friends for so many years,
So many secrets shared,
You wiped away so many tears,
Always the one who cared.
Life has taken us different routes,
You turned left, I turned right,
For a long time I would always look,
Hoping I'd see you in sight.
You were always more mature than me,
Always that one step ahead,
You always took the time to see,
In my life, in my heart, in my head.
The kind of friend without a doubt,
My secrets were safe with you,
So in synch, not a day without,
A day we would talk things through.
I have to admit that up 'til now,
No friendship could ever compare,
I tell myself someway, somehow,
Your memory won't always be there.
You left a number to call you back,
You told me that you were in town,
You thought that maybe we'd backtrack,
Old memories left on the ground.
Part of me wanted to open the door,

(cont'd)

(cont'd)

To start our friendship again,
But then I knew that I'd want more,
And maybe you hadn't changed.
I could already hear the conversation,
A trip down memory lane,
To my troubles you'd make a donation,
To my heart you would add some pain.
So it seems you dropped by yesterday,
You said that you might call again,
I've left a note on my door to say,
You're not welcome, from you I abstain!

CHAPTER CLOSED

I look at my body and still can't believe,
How did I manage to do this to me?
How could I ever stand such pain?
When I harmed myself time and again.
I wanted to scream and I wanted to shout,
I wanted to let my frustration out,
In silence the words would stick in my throat,
Instructing my mouth each time that I spoke.
Holding my tongue, too scared to breathe,
Why bother? I know that they wouldn't believe,
I'm left with these marks to tell me it's true,
What was I thinking? What did I do?
Why did I feel I did not have a choice?
My body screamed out for it was my voice,
Lost in translation they just couldn't see,
This wasn't "attention seeking" for me.
It was simply my way of calming the storm,
That raged inside since the day I was born,
I learned that somehow it helped keep me calm,
It helped me to hide everything that I am.
Ironic I know when I look at myself,
A result of leaving myself on the shelf,
The consequences of trying to hold on,
Not realising I wasn't required to be strong.
Not realising my silence would lead to this,
So anxious and so many moments I'd miss,
So many memories that I never made,
Wearing these marks that might never fade.
I know that I'll never turn the clock back,
I just have to get myself back on track,
I know I don't have to hurt anymore,
I'm finally learning to close that door.

Angela McCrimmon

NON-SENSICAL

How can I start to begin to explain?
To you it will not make sense,
In life there are 2 kinds of pain,
Both hurt but there's one more intense.

You tell me you just cannot equate,
When you hear my desperate scream,
Any compassion will dissipate,
Self-respect you won't let me redeem.

Impatient you tell me to just hold still,
In terror I pull away,
It didn't hurt then but now it will,
In silence I hear what you say.

The pain to which you have to tend,
Is not the real pain at all,
The invisible pain you cannot mend,
And so I continue to fall.

To need your help I feel such shame,
Your resentment you multiply,
You tell me my excuses are lame,
That I have no right to cry.

Often there are times you withhold,
Thinking I'll learn my lesson,
Denying me any pain control,
To reinforce my transgression.

You help my body to all but heal,
Yet you miss where it hurts the most,
The place where I can't bear to feel,
Once again you misdiagnose.

BATTLE SCARS

You may see my scars but you cannot see,
That each one tells a story for me,
A story where I literally fought to survive,
Yet so many times I could have died.
They ask me the triggers and all I can say,
Is that sometimes it helps me get through the day,
Sometimes it helps to make me feel calm,
To quiet my head so that I can...
Present to the world what they want to see,
So I can hide this madness inside of me,
I hide the thoughts that race round my head,
That sometimes I wish I would rather be dead.
I harm because I hurt inside,
My heart and my head seem to collide,
I'm anxious but feel I cannot say,
Because no-one expects me to be this way.
They don't know these wounds I gave to myself,
It was easier to hurt than to ask for help,
These scars tell a story and the story is this,
They're a sign I survived and IT IS WHAT IT IS!

Angela McCrimmon

SUICIDE ISN'T PAINLESS

I've been at this point so many times before,
I'm not sure I can be in this world anymore,
Nothing's ever right, everything is wrong,
Exhausted I can't see the point in holding on.

I've had enough of fighting, I'm tired and I'm weak,
For all that I am talking, some words I just don't speak,
Exhausted and confused, I'm drowning in deep sorrow,
Hoping in my heart I will not be here tomorrow.

I've thought of this so often and I have made my plan,
Ashamed and so guilty to know just what I am,
The phrase "waste of space" is always in my head,
I feel such relief knowing I will soon be dead.

This nightmare will be over, the battle will be done,
I fought against this madness but I guess that it has won,
So drained from the struggle, the struggle to break free,
From the chains and the shackles wrapped around of me.

They're better off without me, I know that this is true,
I feel a little frightened but I know what I must do,
There is no other option, I can see no other way,
"I'm sorry" are the only words I can find to say.

I woke up this morning, I'll admit that I did cry,
I longed to see my loved ones, I longed to say goodbye,
It's time to write my letter but as I picked up my pen,
I realised the pain I felt... I'd just be giving them.

I realise I have to bear my burdens and my strife,
The answers do not lie in the ending of my life,
Suicide is painful for the ones I'd leave behind,
I have to keep on fighting so the strength for them I'll find.

SHAMELESS

You're standing there while her body bleeds,
Desperation in her eyes,
You've made up your mind how you should proceed,
Just send her home to die.

A diagnosis of which you haven't a clue,
The stigma that you attach,
Just be thankful it isn't you,
Because you'd never cope with that!!

Hours to stitch and staple each cut,
You seem so surprised to find,
You look as if to say "Shut up!"
As if it's all in her mind.

I see by your face you're standing by,
The decision you've already made,
You can stand but so will I,
For I know what price will be paid.

I look at her clothes stained in blood,
"Does she look safe to go home??"
She can feel her heart begin to thud,
Your judgement you try to condone.

There's a reason why I'm standing strong,
It's a reason that you'll never see,
It's with you the shame and the doubt belong,
Not with her or with me!!

Angela McCrimmon

DROWNING

I'm sinking deep and I'm sinking fast,
I'm doing my best to swim,
This breath I take could be my last,
I'm losing the strength within.
I'm trying to scream but you don't hear,
Why won't you hear my voice?
You're leaving me with the thing that I fear,
Myself....and I don't have a choice.
I've asked for help and don't understand,
What do you want me to do?
Are you aware that I have made a plan?
I'm terrified I follow it through!
I feel like I'm going over the edge,
There is no soft place to fall,
I'm balancing here on a window ledge,
While you are just watching it all.
Is it just me or is this so unfair?
It feels like I'm the only one,
The only person who seems to care,
That my life isn't over and done.
I know I'm doing the best I can,
Is it enough? I really don't know,
It's like you won't acknowledge I am,
Dying.....and I'm dying slow.

SECRETS AND SHAME

I have to keep my secret for I can't let you see,
I wear my heart underneath my sleeve,
Beneath my clothes you'd find the real me,
The one who only lives because she bleeds.

I'm scared that you would somehow think I've lost my mind,
'Crazy' is the word that you might say,
Sometimes I wish that you could read the signs,
If you did then you might turn away.

I cannot find the words to tell you how I feel,
Frustration eats me up deep inside,
I wonder if my broken heart will ever heal?
Or is it something I'll just have to hide?

I long to tell someone what's really going on,
I'm scared that they just wouldn't believe,
I'm scared that they would tell me what I do is wrong,
I know that but it's not what you perceive.

For now I'll keep my secret for you don't need to know,
I'm scared that you just wouldn't understand,
I wear the pain I'm feeling but I won't let it show,
I just wish I could reach out for your hand.

Angela McCrimmon

YOUR PAIN AND MY PAIN

To anybody else it doesn't make sense,
Why the physical pain could feel so intense,
They're very perplexed and just don't understand,
How these injuries need immediate demand.

They can't comprehend or work out why,
This kind of pain makes us cry,
The answer is simple, why can't they see?
It wasn't intentional, not meant to be.

The pain we inflict is like nothing else,
Not anywhere close if we find ourselves,
With pain that is not ignited by us,
Injuries too painful to even discuss.

When we hurt ourselves we obtain relief,
We hurt to survive, to cope with our grief,
To find ourselves with hurt unintent,
To help us the Drs seem so content.

When the blood is brought on by playing our part,
Stitches repairing a bruised, damaged heart,
That is the illness where they have no respect,
Acknowledge this pain they seem to reject.

Physical or mental....why can't they see?
They're both related, they're both part of me,
They both need help and that's why I beg,
Please treat them the same before I am dead.

WHY??

Why do you not help me? Why will you not stay?
Why will you not listen to a single word I say?
Why won't you acknowledge my sadness or my pain?
Why do you assume all with this label are the same?

Why do you always tell me that I must go straight home?
Why are you quite happy when you know I'll be alone?
Why do you not believe a single word I say?
Why do you discharge me and simply walk away?

Why do you mis-judge me? You know nothing but my name,
Why do you not realise I already feel such shame?
Why do you dismiss me when I'm pleading for your help?
Why do you not realise how much I help myself?

Why do you get angry and say I'm wasting time?
Why can you not see inside this head of mine?
Why will you not answer all the questions saying no?
I guess that the answers I'm never going to know.

Angela McCrimmon

DEAR SELF HARM...

I know we've had this conversation before,
But this time I'm throwing you out the door,
I tried in the past but didn't want to be rude,
For after all you had done me such good.
I appreciate that you've been my friend,
But now I'm afraid it has to end,
I cannot keep you here by my side,
There were times you almost let me die!
There were times when you just went too far,
As if to remind me who you are,
A gentle reminder you're in control,
You hurt my skin and damaged my soul.
I'm stronger now and I can see,
You tried your best to take over me,
No longer will I wear another scar,
To remind me of just who you are.
I'm not ungrateful for I know it's true,
I'm still alive and it's thanks to you,
I know that I wouldn't be standing here,
But the price you charged was just too dear.
I stand here alone and count the cost,
Of all you did and of all I lost,
Memories you thought you had to make,
As another piece of my skin you'd take.
It hurts me we have to say goodbye,
For on you I knew I could always rely,
I know that I'll miss you every day,
But that's why you have to go away.
You've tried to keep me all to yourself,
Didn't want to share me with anyone else,
I can see you now through brand new eyes,
No longer believing all of your lies.
I wish you well but please don't write,
Get out of my mind and out my sight,
To make my point I must confess,
I'm mailed this with no "Return Address."

4
Courage And Conviction

The worst experience of my life turned out to be the best experience. I vowed if I survived I was going to come back fighting with everything I had...and I have! Finally I am finding my voice and the courage to stand up and fight not just for myself, for others who have also found their voice silenced in the system. Mental Health Professionals are going to see that behind the diagnosis, behind the fear to speak out, there was a person. ME.

MY PURPOSE

We live in a world so focused to win,
We see a person but don't look within,
We see a goal and strive right ahead,
Missing out on the journey instead.

Society says that we have to come first,
Drink from the Well, don't wait for the thirst,
Life has no purpose without competition,
I won't enter because this is not my intention.

My intention is to somehow help and to heal,
To give the hurt the permission to feel,
To help the lost find their way home,
To help them see that they're not alone.

I want to help the fallen to stand,
The suicidal unravel their plan,
It's not always life they want to end,
It's the pain they see no way to amend.

To encourage a life that feels so worn,
To mend a heart that's broken and torn,
To listen as if they are all I can hear,
So they can look and know I'm sincere.

I long to help them take back control,
To help them heal their damaged soul,
To empower them so that they can see,
It wasn't so long ago that was me.

Angela McCrimmon

FAITH

I've come so far and struggled through,
It's amazing just what faith can do,
I've searched so high and I've searched so low,
I've been to places I shouldn't go.
I've seen some things that I despise,
My ears have heard a million lies,
There were times I know I lost my way,
Couldn't find the words I had to say.
Yet still my feet kept marching on,
I knew one day this would be gone,
I had to swim against the tide,
Somehow I found the strength inside.
To stand back on these feet of mine,
I believed that there would come a time,
A time when they would look and see,
There's so much more than this to me.
There were times when I couldn't cope,
Yet still my heart clung onto hope,
So many turned and walked away,
It hurt me but I didn't say.
I knew that if I just stayed strong,
One day I'd finally sing my song.

LOST

I've had so many dreams in my life along the way,
Some are with me now and others did not stay,
I can see opportunities but some are so far gone,
Others I can reach if I just keep walking on.

They forget that I still have to work at keeping "well,"
They wouldn't understand so it's a story I don't tell,
I know for myself that being well is still a fight,
Each day a brand new morning followed by the night.

Things they take for granted are things that mean the most,
I walk a narrow line and sometimes the edge is close,
The main thing is keep walking for I will reach my goal,
I know I'm going to get there, I can feel it in my soul.

Leaving my last career to them seems quite insane,
I try to make them see I just don't want to sing again,
They look at me confused because to them it seems so clear,
Singing's what I do and enjoyed year after year.

A change of direction I can see is calling me,
So many inspirations I know that I can be,
My journey's been a challenge, many rivers crossed,
I'm not sure where I'm going but it doesn't mean I'm lost.

Angela McCrimmon

ASSUMPTIONS MISTAKEN

They thought that I didn't want to get well,
No responsibility taken,
My story they just wouldn't let me tell,
And so their assumptions mistaken.

My life they held no expectation,
Clearly they didn't have hope,
No surprise if my own life I'd taken,
So clear to them I couldn't cope.

So many years, their treatment unfair,
No courage to ever speak out,
Hypothesis and only theirs,
My voice I had to live without.

It was evident what they thought of me,
I could see that they held no respect,
They were blind but I could clearly see,
My voice they would always reject.

I made a promise within my heart,
A promise that I would survive,
A promise that I would play a part,
In opening up their eyes!

I know recovery they didn't expect,
I fought with all of my might,
For I knew my story wasn't over yet,
I survived and I'll continue to fight!

WEST LOTHIAN MENTAL HEALTH
ADVOCACY PROJECT

Over the years it's been clear to me,
That sometimes life is unfair,
That's why I needed someone to see,
When my sanity had gone elsewhere.

Injustice was handed to me on a plate,
Along with a fork and knife,
I needed someone to tell me to wait,
When it wanted to eat up my life.

Sometimes step in to help me step out,
To give me some breathing space,
For once I did not need to shout,
Always there with their saving grace.

Common sense when mine had gone,
Hope when I'd left it behind,
Encouragement when I felt I didn't belong,
The genuine, compassionate kind.

So much wisdom to help me trust,
Knowing they'll stand by my side,
Teaching me that in life I must,
Stop feeling I have to hide.

To give me a voice when mine was weak,
To ensure that I got my say,
Patiently waiting for me to speak,
Even when I had lost my way.

Never a judgement, never despair,
Not a hint of frustration shows,
Reassuring and always there,
Even when no-one else knows.

They work so hard behind the scenes,
Advocate when there is no other,
The ones who know how much it means,
To stand up, fight back and recover!

97

Angela McCrimmon

YOU SAID...

You said "You're an inspiration," I look at you confused,
For the words "She's a Drama Queen" are all they ever used.
You said "You have such focus," I wonder what you see?
They said I lack clear goals, don't know where I should be.
You said "You have such courage," I wasn't quite sure how,
For they said I live in fear of the person I am now.
You said "You have such drive," I'm not sure what you know?
They told me I lack purpose and I don't know where to go.
You said "You're very wise," It's a question I must ask,
They said that I am foolish in the present and the past.
You said "You are so brave," I don't feel it half the time,
They said I live in fear of the life that I call mine.
You said "You're going to help," I know this is true,
For I think you know me better than all the others do.

GRATITUDE

I won't sit in sadness at things that I've been through,
I'll turn it all around so I can help others too,
I'll use my own experience to help and understand,
I'll reach out to them when they need to hold a hand.

I'll even be grateful for the lessons I have learned,
I'm thankful for the knowledge I feel that I have earned,
Compassion I will feel, so genuine and true,
Finally comprehending the things I never knew.

I'll help them find the courage to keep fighting on,
The final realization of knowing they are strong,
I'm going to use my strength to show them they can fight,
Help them to believe they can turn the wrong to right.

I'm starting to appreciate the stories I can tell,
I'll understand their sadness for I know it very well,
I'll demonstrate the hope that I know they too can find,
The loneliness I know I can help them leave behind.

I'm thankful for the obstacles that I have overcome,
I'll do my very best to help everyone,
The mountains I have climbed, not sure if I would fall,
The victory I found when I had no faith at all.

Angela McCrimmon

VOICE FROM WITHIN

I heard a little voice today, familiar it is true,
I recognised the spirit in its song,
I couldn't put my finger on exactly how I knew,
But something felt so right where once was wrong.

I knew I could distinguish the difference in its tone,
Similar yet different all the same,
I felt it was a voice that I had always known,
The one that had been silenced in the game.

I listened very closely and stood completely still,
Such volume in the silence I could hear,
This voice I could hear didn't need a pill,
For this voice told me I was not to fear.

I could hear the reassurance and comfort that it brought,
My heart and my head they seemed to slow,
I heard the many words that my soul had ever sought,
The words that told me I already know.

I heard a little voice today, familiar it is true,
I recognised the spirit in its song,
It spoke a little louder, "It's me…yes you,
And I have been here waiting all along."

FIGHT

I've finally found my purpose, the reason I'm alive,
Everything's beginning to make sense,
For all the points of crisis I've managed to survive,
For all the times my suffering was immense.

I've found an understanding that others won't possess,
An empathy of which I now can share,
Accepting in myself that sometimes more is less,
Believing that we never should compare.

I know what it's like to spiral your way down,
So far that you find it hard to breathe,
That's why I'm here to tell that you don't have to drown,
I'm a living testimony to believe.

I'm going to fight for justice for the ones who cannot speak,
I'll stand up and help them have their say,
I'll give them inner strength when they are feeling weak,
When lost I will help them find their way.

I cannot deny that I've been to hell and back,
I will not deny I'd given in,
Destruction where I felt I couldn't backtrack,
Nothing but such fear and guilt within.

I've survived for a reason and I know it is true,
I just should not be standing here today,
I'm here to fight for me and I'm here to fight for you,
I'll fight for us until my dying day.

Angela McCrimmon

SOMETIMES I WONDER

Sometimes I wonder where that girl has gone?
The one that everybody always seen,
The one who would stand up and sing her song,
Confidence was all they ever seen.

Sometimes I wonder where that girl could be?
The one that was striving for a goal,
Heading for stardom, everyone could see,
She sang with every fibre of her soul.

Sometimes I wonder where that girl did go?
The one who truly had so much to give,
The one that was special, did she even know?
She touched so many lives because she lived.

Sometimes I wonder where that girl belongs?
For something in her heart would not reveal,
I could always feel that there was something wrong,
She seemed to feel much more than others feel.

Sometimes I wonder where that girl remains?
Did she ever see her name in lights?
She said that she would make it, they would know her name,
The fire in her soul her dreams ignite.

Sometimes I wonder where that girl has gone?
I look in the mirror and I see,
I realised in that world I did not belong,
I left the stage to find my way to me.

WHO DID I BECOME

It isn't so hard to reflect upon,
The chances come and the chances gone,
After the rain I could see the sun,
But really....who did I become?

Time well spent was time with friends,
The holidays I hoped would never end,
Sometimes empty and feeling so numb,
But really...who did I become?

Trying to speak, my voice shut down,
Ridiculed when no-one else around,
Trapped and with nowhere to turn,
But really...who did I become?

I've become a person with a heartfelt soul,
I've become my purpose, I've found my goal,
I've become someone who will help you up,
I've become someone who will never give up.

I've become this person to love and to care,
I've become this person with so much to share,
I can close my eyes when the day is done,
Knowing I'm proud of who I've become.

Angela McCrimmon

MY PROMISE

I made a promise that if I survived,
If I managed to just pull through,
If somehow I found myself still alive,
I would fight for me and for you!

They wrote me off and let me down,
So many assumptions made,
I couldn't swim, I was left to drown,
The price I have truly paid.

So many nights in that hospital bed,
I begged myself to just breathe,
I'd held on tight and made a pledge,
A pledge that somehow I'd achieve.

I'd achieve the chance to raise my voice,
In a way with composure and calm,
I told myself I would have a choice,
I would make them see who I am!

I'm someone with courage that they couldn't see,
My promise I know I'll fulfil,
They'll open their eyes to see the real me,
I'll fight back and I always will.

OVERLOOKED

I was left not feeling I had any choice,
Now it seems that I'm finding my voice,
No-one would listen to my explanations,
My voice will be heard across the nations.

Never one to do things by half,
I've excelled myself and I can't help but laugh,
For the irony of so many years,
Scared into silence, left with such fears.

They looked at me and assumptions were made,
For their neglect I know I have dearly paid,
Repeatedly told it was all in my mind,
Their care and compassion left far behind.

So many times I tried to express,
I honestly felt they couldn't care less,
Some clearly did but I'm afraid that most,
Would push me away instead of draw close.

They can look at me now if that's what they choose,
They'll see I am fighting and I will not lose,
Determined and focused that's what they'll see,
If they'd looked past the label they would have found me.

Angela McCrimmon

READY OR NOT

Life it seems is crazy, but crazy kind of good,
Finally things are turning out the way they should,
Finally I'm standing right where I should be,
I'm ready but I question is the world ready for me?

I see my dreams ahead and I'm heading straight for them,
I never gave up trying even when they did condemn,
When things never changed, I just kept walking on,
Sometimes my head fell down but my hope was never gone.

My voice it had been silenced but my song I'm going to sing,
I failed to understand but I learned from everything,
I told myself the lessons that I always had to learn,
Were the ones from which I know my self- respect was earned.

Opportunities it's true are coming fierce and fast,
You'll see me walk in front, no longer coming last,
I never stopped believing even when they put me down,
I picked myself back up, never staying on the ground.

So take these words and please remember what I say,
I'm looking to the future, I'm not stuck in yesterday,
You'll see I have more courage than any of you thought,
Look out world... here I come.....ready or not!!

CONTROL

They control every move I make,
Each mile I walk, each step I take,
They take my voice so I can't say,
My opinion's worthless anyway.

They control what I dare dream,
So much to the eye unseen,
So much I can never tell,
They hide the evidence so well.

They control what they dictate,
They tell me pills I have to take,
If I should dare to not comply,
They don't care if I live or die.

They control what others see,
They shift the blame, they say it's me,
They say I bring it on myself,
That I'm to blame and no-one else.

They DON'T control my beating heart,
They have NO say in where I start,
They have NO say in where I go,
They never have, I just didn't know.

Angela McCrimmon

MEDICAL MADNESS

I cannot believe I am standing here today,
I stand here and I hold my head up high,
For all the times you turned and walked away,
For all the times you left me there to cry.

You saw a diagnosis, a label just to show,
The sort of patient I was going to be,
"Professional" yet you still didn't know,
The label I was wearing wasn't me.

I'm not saying your diagnosis was wrong,
It's your treatment that really broke my heart,
You made it very clear that I did not belong,
Predicted the end result before the start.

I came to you for help, sometimes a little late,
You've no idea the strength it took to come,
Hours in A&E you always made me wait,
As if to dissuade my next return.

I hated being there, you seemed to miss that part,
So caught up in the theories you believed,
I didn't try to speak for my own voice did depart,
I knew my place and all that you perceived.

I'm so privileged to be given this chance to have a voice,
To help you see you've so much to discover,
You need to understand we don't always have a choice,
Sometimes we need your help to just recover.

Maybe you are thinking that I'm wasting your time,
Bet hey.....I guess that's nothing new!
But maybe if you looked beyond this label of mine,
I might just look beyond yours too!

DON'T GIVE UP

Some might say I'm stubborn, I'm not sure if that's true,
You have your opinion but I have got mine too,
You're not living in my head, you don't hear it say,
The voice that says "Don't dare give up you'll make it soon someday."

Some might say I'm weak, I'm not sure if that's true,
I know how much strength it takes to keep on pushing through,
I know the spirit inside me that keeps me fighting on,
The one that says "Don't dare give up someday this will be gone."

Some might say I'm cowardly, I'm not sure if that's true,
I have much more courage than I know some others do,
I know how much bravery I practice every day,
The kind that says "Don't dare give up somehow you'll find a way."

Some might say I'm crazy, I'm not sure if that's true,
I don't think that I am any crazier than you,
It's not hallucinations when I say I hear a voice,
The one that says "Don't dare give up coz you don't have a choice!!"

Some might say I'm foolish, I'm not sure if that's true,
I have much more wisdom than you expect me to,
I have more understanding than you could ever know,
The kind that says "Don't dare give up you haven't far to go."

Angela McCrimmon

I SIT

I sit here in my silence for I cannot convey,
The words that I long for you to hear,
I sit here discouraged as I watch you walk away,
Your footsteps in the distance I now fear.
I sit here with heartache for I can feel the pain,
It seems as if you try to break my heart,
I come to the conclusion that you are all the same,
You've assumed the end before I even start.
I sit here in wonder at the things you do not see,
It's hard for me to truly comprehend,
I wish I had the boldness to say "Hey look at me!!"
But I'm too scared the message that would send.
I sit here frustrated for I know it's been so long,
I don't think you have ever understood,
Instead you sit in judgement telling me I'm wrong,
Giving me the message I'm no good.
I sit here so confused at why you cannot see,
It's not attention I am trying to seek,
You seem to think that this is all I'll ever be,
Your "tough love" just leaves me feeling weak.
I sit here contemplating not sure what to do,
It's like you think it's your right to demand,
Respect from me, but I see now it's true,
No longer will I sit, I choose to stand!

MY COMEBACK FROM CRAZY

I opened my book today, the story of my life,
So much has happened that I know I have to write,
Another chapter in it, I need to add another page,
It seems that my vocabulary is becoming my new stage.

I took some time to read the words I wrote before,
I picked up my pen so I could write a little more,
It seems I'm on a journey and although I don't know where,
When I reach my destination I know that I'll be there.

So many memories so scared I might forget,
So many people I'm so glad that I have met,
So many special moments we've shared along the way,
I want to write them down, I'll look back on them one day.

I realised as I write that some memories were sad,
I realised I had lost some of the people that I had,
I paused for a moment as a tear fell from my eyes,
It smudged the ink a little when I remembered our goodbyes.

I smiled as I recalled the laughter and the smiles,
How I'd kept walking though my journey had been miles,
I'd turned another corner as I'd reached another goal,
I'd claimed back the self- respect insanity had stole.

I read over what I'd written and I put down my pen,
I'd written my last chapter though I hadn't known it then,
I've come back from many things but I know that it's true,
I've "Comeback From Crazy" and I know that you can too.

Angela McCrimmon

HOLDING HANDS

I always thought being strong meant doing it on my own,
Too scared to ask for kindness despite all I'd been shown,
I didn't want to burden anyone in my life,
I tried my best to handle my own pain and my own strife.

We all have our Dr's but I know we're all the same,
We do not take the time or don't want to complain,
I thought that if I waited my storm would surely pass,
Although I often wondered how long that it would last.

I didn't want to tell them for fear they'd disbelieve,
I figured if they didn't then what would that achieve?
I figured I'd be better to just keep marching on,
I didn't really notice my soul was all but gone.

It was only really after I had truly broken down,
The nights I'd spend crying with no-one else around,
The nights I spent screaming, praying it would stop,
I had to learn a lesson and it's one I've not forgot.

Courage is being brave enough to let somebody in,
Daring to be honest when you feel such doubt within,
Reaching for that hand when you want so much to be,
Far away from everyone so no-one else can see.

I had to teach myself for I really didn't know,
How to ask for help or even where to go,
If I can teach that lesson now for anyone to hear,
I'd say "Please find the courage" for I am standing here.

PASSION AND PURPOSE

They ask me what's my passion, what really stirs my soul?
I wasn't sure the answer I should give,
I took the time to ask myself what truly is my goal?
What is the kind of life I want to live?

Within my self- reflection I realised it is true,
There's one thing that really holds my heart,
I want to reach the hurting, those like me and you,
Those who feel their life's been torn apart.

I've lived through many things not sure I'd survive,
So much of myself I'd hide away,
Help me to show you I'm now happy I'm alive,
I'm thankful I am standing here today.

I've done so many courses and learned so many skills,
I always used to question why I do?
It may not make much sense but I know one day it will,
For I am going to share these skills with you.

I had to learn my lessons so that I could teach,
Others that there is another way,
In that education maybe I could reach,
Those who need to hear "you'll be okay."

So yes, I've found my passion, it was there all along,
I knew that when I found it I would know,
My heart is for the hurting who aren't always strong,
To tell them "YES" when all they've heard is "NO."

Angela McCrimmon

SERENITY

I think when you have lived a life of fear,
You appreciate the little things,
Like even the fact you're standing here,
Or can take to the sky with your wings.

No anxiety to hold you back,
A peacefulness felt within,
The confidence you always lacked,
Comfortable in your own skin.

No thoughts racing around your head,
Intoxicating your mind,
A feeling of serenity instead,
That you never thought you'd find.

You finally know that you can dream,
For your faith won't let you down,
You stand up tall for it truly seems,
Your heart will not hit the ground.

No longer obsessed by what they think,
Their thoughts are not yours to claim,
Not walking a line close to the brink,
So terrified you've gone insane.

Finally feeling you've turned a page,
A new story you have to write,
No hanging around behind backstage,
It's time to be in the spotlight.

HAPPY NEW YEAR

To be honest I'm finding it hard to believe,
How people are being inspired by me,
I always knew my life was bizarre,
But I cannot believe I've come this far.
A year ago I was almost dead,
Another operation instead,
Another attempt I will not lie,
For most of me just wanted to die.
I couldn't predict by the end of the year,
I'd have made it through to be standing here,
A story to tell how I fought to survive,
A story to say thank God I'm alive!
So much is happening at the same time,
I stand in awe at this life of mine,
Full circle, 360 degrees,
A sense of relief, I'm finally free.
My heart is to help those in pain,
I need them to see that I was the same,
So broken down, now standing tall,
I need them to know if ever they fall.
There's someone who will understand,
Help before things get out of hand,
The road to ruin is a slippery slope,
They need to reach out, take the rope.
I don't want my struggle to be in vain,
If it's not then it's been worth the pain,
Encouragement is surrounding me,
Their kind words are reminding me.
There are people out there with a sincere heart,
Happy New Year, it's a brand new start!

Angela McCrimmon

SINCERE SMILE

You always see me smiling and these days it's sincere,
You often say it brightens up your day,
I guess it's because I am happy to be here,
My insanity finally went away.

You say I'm always happy and I guess that it's true,
Any sadness I feel does not last long,
I feel proud when I look at what I've come through,
Knowing I have proved so many wrong.

I discovered the strength that lies within me,
Now I know I always can defeat,
Any challenges that I might ever see,
Any adversity I'll ever meet.

You don't know my reasons when you hear me say,
The cliche words "life's too short,"
I thank God for my own every single day,
For many times I tried to abort.

I hope that it's true and you do get what you give,
For I know I'm going to give my very best,
I want to make a difference with the life that I live,
For I can see I truly have been blessed.

SILENCE IS GOLDEN

I keep my silence but please don't assume,
That I don't have much to say,
I have more than enough, I don't let it consume,
Each minute of my waking day.

I see much more than you think I do,
But I choose to turn away,
The truth is I have a birds eye view,
There's so much that I don't say.

I truly think there's a lot to be said,
For the power that no words can say,
Sometimes I like to be quiet instead,
In silence the message convey.

The words so often race through my mind,
But often I don't let them out,
If you pause to read between the lines,
You'll see why there's no need to shout.

The next time you think that you cannot hear,
My voice, don't think that I hide,
There's a lot I could say for I do not fear,
I just know when to keep it inside.

YOU MAY...

You may have torn me down but I know I'll get back up,
My glass is just half full but I'll add another cup.
You may have drained my strength but I know I will regain,
My courage and my spirit to start to fight again.
You may have left me feeling so lonely and so lost,
I will find direction no matter what the cost.
You may have pushed me over but I know that I will stand,
I'll walk on solid ground, no longer in quicksand.
You may have left me wondering and not sure what do,
I no longer sit in question, for I see I always knew.
You may have left me feeling frustrated and in tears,
No longer will I let you add to all my fears.
You may have left me cold and out there in the storm,
I'm ready for the sunshine, the rain will all be gone.
You may have left me feeling so misunderstood,
I'll understand myself like I never thought I could.
You may think I am weak but what you do not see,
The deep determination that burns inside of me.
You may think I'm not worth your trouble or your time,
Keep your own opinion because I am keeping mine.
You may think I'll never find a place where I belong,
Doubt me?...Just watch me...cause I'm going to prove you wrong!!!

5
PS...

I want to leave the readers on a lighter note with some poems I'm sure you will resonate with and some that might even make you smile. If there's any huge factor that's helped me survive living with Mental Illness it's my sense of humour. Even in my darkest times I can usually still find something that makes me smile. Amidst a thunderstorm I know that if I just keep walking, the sun will shine again...and it always does.

WEATHER REPORT

Moods are like the weather changing every day,
Some stay for a season and other just a day,
Some people like summer, others like the spring,
What matters most is whatever joy they bring.

When I feel like Autumn I'm feeling rather free,
It's like I'm shedding worries like the trees shed their leaves,
The thing I find with Autumn is I'm sort of in-between,
The summer and the winter if you know just what I mean.

When I feel like winter I can act a little cold,
It's not my intention but it's true or so I'm told,
The thing I find with winter is that I am more aware,
There seems to be a little sadness everywhere.

Moods are like the weather changing every day,
I know the spring and summer are almost on the way,
I realise that the weather lives inside of me,
And I can choose the season whatever that might be.

Angela McCrimmon

RISKY BUSINESS

We're too afraid to take a risk for fear that we might fail,
We refuse to jump on board too afraid we might derail,
We seem to live our lives with only half a heart,
We feel the negativity before we even start.

We try to see the "pros" but we know we always do,
See the "cons" more clearly so we don't follow through,
We keep our hopes and dreams locked up in a box,
They'll be safe in there… or at least that's what we thought.

Life is just too risky so we prefer to step on back,
We don't see what we have, only see the things we lack,
We see the possibility that things could all go wrong,
For fear that we might drown we prefer to float along.

Hope may sometimes hurt but it's worth every pain,
For life gives one chance and it won't come round again,
Take every risk and hold onto your dreams,
You'll see the risk you take is not as scary as it seems.

A LESSON LEARNED

I learned how to earn a person's respect,
By being proud of all the lives I have wrecked.
I learned how to trust and always believe,
By assuring I always set out to deceive.
I learned how to love and never to hurt,
By making so sure that I hurt them first.
I learned to find peace at the end of each day,
By pushing them all right out the way.
I learned how to laugh and always to smile,
By pleasing myself, no-one else was worthwhile.
I learned to succeed no matter the cost,
By working myself to the point I exhaust.
I learned that to win is always what should,
By realising that 2nd best is no good.
I learned how to take good care of myself,
By treating myself with my money and wealth.
I learned how to love the body God gave,
By skipping my meals so I could save.
I learned to accept and to never condone,
By criticising each person I've known.
You taught many lessons that helped to mould me,
By showing the person I don't want to be.

Angela McCrimmon

TEARS

Tears can be happy or tears can be sad,
To embrace the good or regret the bad,
They can be a sure sign of letting go,
Trusting your heart when your head says no.

Tears can show wisdom where there is no sense,
Releasing the angst from where you feel tense,
Releasing frustration when you want to scream,
Or when you are frightened awake from a dream.

Tears show compassion where there is cruel,
Tugging your heartstrings, push and then pull,
Sometimes we are forced to live with regret,
Accepting it's time to forgive and forget.

Tears say hello and tears say goodbye,
We watch life be born and we watch life die,
Sometimes we wonder if it's worth the pain,
Then something happens and we smile again.

Tears say I love you when there are no words,
They help us make sense of what seems absurd,
They say they're a sign that you've held on too long,
So just cry and know you don't have to be strong.

CURRICULUM VITAE

Flicking through the paper an advert caught my eye,
I hesitated slightly as I almost read right by,
"Space Cadets required all across the nation,"
The job was made for me so I sent off my application.

"Experience Required"... I guess that's where to start,
I knew if nothing else I definitely had that,
I'd achieved many medals in my journey on the way,
A "Professional Cadet" I guess that you could say.

"Most Recent Employment"... well technically it's true,
Not a day of unemployment, break well overdue,
I haven't had a sick day in at least 20 years,
Dedication and commitment to serve up with my fears.

It said to state my "Strengths,"... I had to pick and choose,
The winning streak I had was that I never failed to lose,
I knew the road to stardom, almost always on my way,
I'd simply been diverted when the roadworks had delayed.

It asked "My Life Ambition"... what did I dare to dream?
Had I held the future when the past was all I seen?
Had I kept my focus even when I couldn't tell?
If I was going to end up in heaven or in hell.

"Personal Statement"... I think this is where I,
Stand by my conviction and show how hard I try,
With rock hard perseverance and hope beyond compare,
The proof was in the picture with many marks still there.

"2 References Required"...this may take some time,
I'd have to pick the right ones to make sure they align,
They need to represent the job to which applied,
I need to get this right or they might think I've lied.

"Other Relevant Information"...I could be here a while,
I began to realise and as I did I smiled,
They were looking for a Space Cadet, calling out across the nation,
The job's already mine so I withdrew my application.

Angela McCrimmon

STRANGERS

Would it be okay if I sat here for a while?
Maybe we could contemplate together?
Others may not notice but I can see your smile,
Its sincerity has changed just like the weather.

I know you do not know me but maybe this is why,
You can talk to me and open up your heart,
At the end of this conversation we can say goodbye,
Our time will end and we can both depart.

I know that you are hurting , I see it in your eyes,
I see a true reflection just like mine,
Why do you tell me that yourself you do despise?
I pray that you will love yourself in time.

I genuinely care so please feel free to talk,
Not one sense of judgement will you find,
You think that I'm "together" but maybe I am not,
That's why I see the turmoil in your mind.

You say you often feel like no-one understands,
I ask if you have given them the chance?
You tell me you're drowning so fast in quicksand,
Rational and insanity in a dance.

You stand up from the seat and thank me for my time,
You see your is bus coming up ahead,
I'll be here tomorrow, the same place and time,
I won't repeat a single word you've said.

PRO-ACTIVE

I've always been "Pro-active"...To me it's the only way,
I'm the only one who can orchestrate my day,
Some of what might happen in my life is down to me,
And other things will happen but I always hold the key.

We know there are some things and others we don't do,
It's finding the discernment to separate the two,
I've always tried to be the stirrer of my pot,
So I know what's going in and what I have forgot.

I've tried to climb my mountain but I always fall back down,
I guess I'm often reckless so I end up on the ground,
Some lessons I learn quick while others I take time,
Whatever reckless card I play that mountain still needs climbed.

Never one to stay down long, I get back up and fight,
I fight with everything I have to try and make things right,
I've done all the training and I was ready for my race,
I couldn't understand why defeat was in my face.

There's a lot to be said to look inside yourself,
I have every "self-help" book ever sitting on my shelf,
I've followed their 12 step program and every other rule,
I half expect the last page to scream "HA.....APRIL FOOL!"

Among my many travels, some up but mostly down,
I've swum over mighty waves when I thought that I would drown,
My life came with no roadmap but I guess that time did tell,
The journey has been worth it, I had to know I was as well.

Angela McCrimmon

INSOMNIA

Does anyone else lie awake at night?
Silently putting the world to rights,
Wondering if they should get out of bed,
Or keep on trying to sleep instead.

It's December and I seem to think it's funny,
To think about the Easter Bunny,
The January sales will start next week,
My kitchen ceiling's beginning to leak.

I must remember I need to shop,
Afraid to starve then realise I'm not,
Slim or in danger of fading away,
Maybe I'll start my diet today?

I'm sure I seen dust on the table,
I think I'll get up while I am able,
I guess I might as well vacuum too,
I know I've got so much to do.

I wonder what is on TV?
I'll turn it on, so I can see,
Ooh I like this programme on,
Oops, another hour has gone!

I'll start Xmas shopping online,
A year early, it'll be on time,
Amazon maybe or a bid on Ebay,
I'm a little worried what I must pay.

I start to feel like I'm slowing down,
My head is no longer spinning around,
I decide to climb back into bed,
Then realise it's time to get up instead!!

LOVE

Love someone for just being who they are,
It's not about the job or whatever fancy car.
Love without a reason other than to care,
It's not about the motive or agenda that is there.
Love with true compassion so they will always feel,
The smile that you give them is genuine and real.
Love without judgement, opinions can be kept,
Listen if they're talking, don't try to intercept.
Love with your own boundaries so that they will see,
How to set their own and the way that things should be.
Love without taking for you are there to give,
They may not have seen there's any other way to live.
Love with acceptance to show them it's okay,
To be just who they are, no need to turn away.
Love without apology so they know you're sincere,
If they pull away just show them you're still here.
Love with understanding, make them feel worthwhile,
For maybe in their life no-one's gone the extra mile.

Angela McCrimmon

DVD OF MY LIFE

I pressed PLAY and my life began to start,
The moments in my life had begun,
Each minute passed by, each beat of my heart,
A smile to give everyone.

I pressed FAST FORWARD so desperate to see,
Exactly what my life had in store,
Would it be everything I hoped it would be?
Or would I be left wanting more?

I hit REWIND this wasn't the plan,
I'm met with such doubt and disdain,
This isn't the person I know that I am,
Can I press the START button again?

I pressed EJECT I knew there were things,
In my life that just had to go,
I'd realised the sadness that they bring,
And how much I just didn't know.

In that moment I realised that I'd forgot,
I'd forgot because I didn't know how,
I'd forgot to PAUSE never gave it a thought,
I need to live in the right here and now.

So back at the START but I know that this time,
Will be different than it was before,
I've pressed Fast Forward, Pause and Rewind,
No need to EJECT anymore.

MY MAKE-UP BAG

I'll start with foundation for this provides my base,
It helps hide each blemish I find upon my face,
It smooths out any wrinkles, it softens up my skin,
I need to match the shade and then I shall begin.

I need to pick eyeshadow, which colour shall I choose?
The colours are so vital to ensure that they diffuse,
This is my key feature just to open up my eyes,
When I'm feeling dead inside this makes me look alive.

A little touch of blusher is most definitely required,
It gives a gentle glow when I am feeling tired,
A picture of health is what my blusher always shows,
So that way if I'm not then no-one else will know.

My eyes will need mascara, each lash it does extend,
My eyes appear engaging so a message they can send,
The message that I'm ready and that I invite your gaze,
When I wear mascara my disguise can always stay.

I need to check my make up so I can take a look,
I cannot fail to notice that for all the time it took,
There's still a little spot in need of some correction,
I take out my concealer to perfect my own complexion.

The next stage is the last for it's where my story ends,
It's the final declaration of the memo that it sends,
My lipstick choice is vital for it compliments my face,
Now I can face the world because my make-up is in place.

Angela McCrimmon

MY BUCKET LIST

I saw it in a movie once, the person made a list,
All the things he wants to do and all the things he missed,
It really got me thinking what my list would be,
I wondered what hope and dreams I held inside of me?

I've always said I'd love to throw myself out of a plane,
That sounds a little drastic and to some I guess insane,
I love the thought of flying so high above the clouds,
Freedom for that moment where no thoughts are allowed.

I've always fancied travelling, Australia my first stop,
Then onto Singapore or maybe island hop,
I'd love to see Hawaii or Barbados even more,
Discover other cultures and what they have in store.

Maybe I could visit all my family and friends?
Some in John O'Groats and others at Lands End,
I miss them all so much and the memories we made,
I'd love to make some new ones though the old will never fade.

I've dreamed about a jet-ski where waves crash around,
I'd find a desert island where I wouldn't hear a sound,
I'd stay there for the night, I'd build my own camp fire,
Staring at the skies and the stars I would admire.

I paused for a moment as I realised there's one thing,
I'd forsake all the dreams I have, I'd forsake everything,
My dreams could last forever and the hope will always stay,
I scored out all that's on my list and told myself I'd pray.

I wouldn't pray for flying or travelling Far East,
I wouldn't dream of beaches, no camp fire or a feast,
No bucket list required, only one thing that I ask,
My mental health restored and may that restoration last.

PEOPLE

We meet many people but not all of them stay,
Some forever, others just a day,
God will send them for as long as we need,
To help us bloom by planting a seed.

Each person brings with it a lesson to learn,
Sometimes they teach us how to discern,
Learning can hurt when we don't understand,
Further ahead we realise we can.

Some come with a smile when we need it most,
A reminder of who in our life to pull close,
Admitting that sometimes we need to let go,
Trust there are answers even when we don't know.

We learn how to earn our trust and respect,
From reacting in life when we feel reject,
Don't sink to a level we want to destruct,
Take a step back and more pain we'll deduct.

Some come in love though others in fear,
Each at a cost the price can be dear,
Some are priceless and these are the ones,
To never let go of no matter what comes.

Angela McCrimmon

DISCRIMINATION

They say "1 out of four" will experience it too,
Mental illness they mean, I know that it's true,
I look at my friends and I wonder if they see,
That "1 out of 4" sadly now is me.

People joke around, I try to laugh along,
I hope they cannot see that my smile has all but gone,
The smile that they see isn't real at all,
I've drawn it on my face and prayed it wouldn't fall.

They say "He's so mental" and laugh at his expense,
I wish that I was brave so I could come to his defence,
I wish I felt so strong that I really could stand up,
But I know when I fall I can barely get back up.

"He's escaped from the loony bin", I hear that all the time,
If only they realised that this story could be mine,
That "loony bin" they speak of, I've only just got out,
On the outside I'm silent but inside I try to shout!

"He's not right in the head", I hang my own in shame,
If they knew my secret they would say I'm just the same,
For fear they'd see the truth I feel I have to lie,
For fear they'd run a mile shouting back "Goodbye."

A girl walks by, they mock and shout "You're mad!"
I smile at her gently for I see that she is sad,
I empathise so deeply though I'm glad they cannot see,
If they want "madness" they need only look at me.

"1 out of 4" that's what experts say,
In that very moment it was clear to me that they,
All looked a bit uneasy, in that moment I could see,
Each one said in a whisper "I think that one is me."

The moral of this story I think is very clear,
Each person has a story that brought them right to here,
Each person has a story, it's simple and it's true,
Mental health does not discriminate between me and you.

MY PRAYER

There are some prayers you never think you will pray,
You struggle to find the right words to say,
You search in your heart, you search in your soul,
They tell me in Him to step out and be bold.

They tell me He'll listen if I ever speak,
He'll give me hope when things look so bleak,
He will reassure me that things are okay,
He will bring me back when I walk away.

I tell myself "Well, I'll give it a go,"
I hear Him remind me I already know,
He's shown me so many times in the past,
He'll answer my prayer if only I'd ask....

"Dear Lord, he is weary, his body in pain,
His memory fails him time and again,
He looks so scared, so lost and alone,
Won't you please come and take him back home?
Lord I am asking please won't you be,
Close to him and set his heart free,
His body so frail it's hard to believe,
He holds my hand when I try to leave.
Once so strong and now is so frail,
His mind so sharp, now his memory fails,
I'm there but I wonder does he even know?
He looks so sad when I turn to go.
I don't know how much he does understand,
The only comfort I can give is my hand,
Locked in his world, he cannot speak,
Once so strong and now is so weak.
I pray you will comfort him day after day,
When he's lost somehow you'll show him the way,
I can see him drift, his mind disappear,
When he's scared I pray that you'll draw him near.

(Cont'd)

135

(Cont'd)

Each time I see him, I know in my heart,
That time's running out, I knew from the start,
I knew that this illness would take him from me,
So soon, so quick, it's hard to believe.
Lord I am asking that you will protect,
For a moment I plead "please don't take him yet!"
One look I can see that he doesn't have long,
I wonder if he knows that something is wrong?
These questions could haunt me so I know I must,
Remind myself in you I must trust,
I pray that he's sitting with you by your throne,
Dear Lord, I pray... please come take him home."

STARTING OVER

My life is kinda crazy, I'm sure you would agree,
I have no explanation for what it throws at me,
The many situations it seems that I do find,
Myself in the centre, the astonishing kind.

I look around at others and fail to see the same,
Insanity in their life, mine seems like a game,
A game of win or lose, a game of in or out,
I stand back in awe at what my life is all about.

Opportunities coming and as crazy as they are,
Some are unexpected, most are just bizarre,
So much can happen in just one single day,
I truly never know what life will throw my way.

I wonder what is "normal" as I dare to contemplate,
Could I start my life over or is it just too late?
The question I guess that is always in my head,
Would I want to be me or someone else instead?

I already know the answer so I'm not sure why I ask,
I see inside my heart although sometimes wear a mask,
I see that I am "different" sometimes my life's insane,
But if I could start over, I'd do it all over again.

Angela McCrimmon

CHILD FOR A DAY

Today I decided that I would try,
To remember when I was a child,
Sometimes bold, sometimes shy,
And most definitely totally wild!

I thought I'd choose to live today,
As if I were very young,
To see the world in just that way,
So this is what I have done…

I skipped along in the tall green grass,
As I sang my favourite song,
I began to run so very fast,
Laughing as I raced along.

I sat down to play with a buttercup,
I held it right under my chin,
It would tell me if I liked butter or not,
I'm not sure, couldn't see my skin.

I spotted a dandelion and thought,
I must blow it gently to see,
He loves me yes, he loves me not,
I made sure he always loved me.

I went to the park and sat on a swing,
I giggled as I ran about,
I did not care about anything,
I span fast on the roundabout.

(Cont'd)

(Cont'd)

I found some pocket money I'd earned,
I decided to go to the shop,
I wasn't even slightly concerned,
When I'd happily spent the lot.

I froze for a moment, scared to look,
I looked at this watch of mine,
I'm not sure how much time it took,
But I made it back for teatime.

As I ate my chicken nuggets and fries,
I sipped my juice from my cup,
My childhood I'd had a taste of this,
Why did I ever grow up?

Angela McCrimmon

CONTEMPLATING

What would I do if I didn't have my words?
Where would all my feelings go?
Maybe some people find me quite absurd?
But that's the only way I seem to know.

It seems that things that fill up my mind,
All the things I feel within my heart,
This is where all the healing I can find,
The place I come when things might fall apart.

Maybe I'm too open, uneasiness you feel?
If this is true I don't apologise,
I'm only being honest, I'm simply being real,
For all my life's been hidden in such lies.

Maybe you should try it, open up inside,
Allow yourself to truly understand,
Give yourself permission, there's no need to hide,
Your heart and head with silence you command.

JUST BE STILL

So scared I'll miss one moment that I make so many plans,
Determined to stand up and show them who I am,
Lessons I should learn but don't think I ever will,
Somewhere in my head a voice says... "Just be still."

Manically I seem to race right through the day,
Grabbing opportunities that ever come my way,
Adrenaline rushes and I can feel the thrill,
Somewhere in my head a voice says... "Just be still."

People keep asking me to do so many things,
I cannot deny all the happiness that brings,
Unhappiness I'll say I've truly had my fill,
Somewhere in my head a voice says... "Just be still."

I can feel excitement as it rushes through my veins,
Anticipation strong for what the day contains,
I need to slow my mind or I risk my getting ill,
Somewhere in my head a voice says... "Just be still."

Angela McCrimmon

RECIPE FOR ANGELA

A little pinch of madness to compliment a smile,
A tablespoon of strength to walk on another mile,
Mix in a little courage so you can win each fight,
This is the key ingredient so you must get it right.

Find a pen and paper to write instructions down,
Morning, noon or night when words need to be found,
You can write them anytime for what you think or feel,
These instructions are authentic, each word your heart reveals.

Bake for 20 mins at 200 degrees,
Prepare a plate of wisdom, a side dish if you please,
Cool it with some insight to mix with medication,
This part must be perfect for this is the foundation.

Another cup of wisdom and leave it overnight,
Check it in the morning for you must get it right,
A Kilo of persistence, such deep determination,
Faith that God can handle any given situation.

Mix it all together and have a little taste,
No need for perfection, just don't put it to waste,
So here we have a recipe for you and all to see ,
Shake it up, add some fizz and now you've "bottled" me.

Lightning Source UK Ltd.
Milton Keynes UK
UKOW05f0733151116
287623UK00003B/929/P